Andrea's book, Intentional Living, *will* but to act. *This book is about intentional* affect the kingdom of God, just as Jesus ... in God's power. *You will realize God is counting on your choices and His power to impact His kingdom today as you read stories of how that happens, through ordinary people. When I am with Andrea Mullins, I am drawn into Christ's presence. She radiates Him. One quickly recognizes her intentional lifestyle and passion for making a difference in her world, and she challenges you to do the same.*

—Esther Burroughs
author of *Engraved by Grace*
and *Treasures of a Grandmother's Heart*

Living the Christlike life does not happen automatically; it is a choice we make each day. No one knows this better than Andrea Mullins, who has spent a lifetime choosing to follow God's way for her life. Through Scripture, stories, and her own life experiences, Andrea challenges each of us to experience life to the fullest by intentionally living for the Lord every day.

—Wanda Lee
Executive Director, Woman's Missionary Union

Jesus the Christ lived and died to make us fit for the kingdom—a gift of grace. To live effectively as a citizen of God's kingdom, however, is a choice. Andrea Mullins makes a strong case for every Christ follower living intentionally for God's purposes. Andrea brings head and heart together, focusing on principles of intentionality that play themselves out in her own life experiences and those of fellow believers she has encountered around the world. She affirms that intentional followers of Christ can become intentional leaders who continually validate the journey of faith, wholeness, and commitment to the glory of God.

—Dr. Bill O'Brien
founding director of the Global Center at Samford University and
codirector of BellMitra Associates, and
—Dr. Dellanna O'Brien
former Executive Director, Woman's Missionary Union
and codirector of BellMitra Associates

INTENTIONAL
LIVING

CHOOSING to LIVE for GOD'S PURPOSES

IntenTional
Living

ANDREA
JONES MULLINS

new
hope
PUBLISHERS
Birmingham, Alabama

New Hope® Publishers
P. O. Box 12065
Birmingham, AL 35202-2065
www.newhopepublishers.com

Library of Congress Cataloging-in-Publication Data
Mullins, Andrea Jones, 1948-
   Intentional living : choosing to live for God's purposes / Andrea
Jones Mullins.
      p. cm.
   ISBN 1-56309-927-6 (softcover)
   1. Christian life. I. Title.
   BV4501.3.M852 2005
   248.4--dc22

                                                       2005013714

ISBN: 1-56309-927-6
N054116•0905•4.5M1

Dedication

To Michele, Michael, Chelsea, Patrick, and Nicolas

*Michele, your compassion humbles me—I am honored to be
your mother*
Michael, your love is a gift to all of us
Chelsea, your prayers encourage me to believe
Patrick, your courage strengthens me to be bold
Nicolas, you make me laugh with delight

Your growing faith brings me the greatest joy.
May every day be about Jesus—
Who He is, how He loves you, and what He has for you to do.
I love you.

*"And may the Master pour on the love so it fills your lives
and splashes over on everyone around you, just as it does
from us to you."*

—1 Thessalonians 3:12 (*The Message*)

TABLE OF CONTENTS

INTRODUCTION

CHOOSING TO LIVE FOR GOD'S PURPOSES

When I arrived in an unfamiliar city where I was speaking, I accidentally took several wrong turns. But the next thing I knew, I was right where I had intended to go! Fortunately for me, the turns I chose eventually ended up right where I wanted to be. Choosing to live for God's purposes doesn't happen in this same way. We must make an intentional decision to go where God leads in order to end up where God wants us to go.

My grandson Patrick decided as a young boy to be intentional about his faith. One day while waiting with his mother to get his sister from school, Patrick said, "I love Jesus, and I want to be baptized right now." Now, as an early teen, Patrick is continuing his intentional commitment to Christ. Recently he emailed me to tell me that he had struggled in his faith. "I didn't really think that God was there. I thought that He was nothing and that I was nothing. I then went to a summer camp with my church. I had a great time and I really liked it. Then one night I went to my youth leader and he realized how I felt and told me that he went through the same thing I was going through. Now I feel like there is something there. I no longer feel like nothing." Patrick will find that this soul searching and renewing of his faith is an intentional journey of recommitment to God that will continue throughout his life.

A feature on today's computers is the choice to let them go into hibernation if they aren't used for a while. Hibernation is a power-saving option. In my own journey I've found myself choosing to hibernate rather than allow God's power to transform me enough to transform the world around me. But when I awaken to God's purposes, I discover a renewed joy in living. Like Patrick, I need help from God and from my fellow believers to continue to realize that I have value and that God cares for me.

Some years ago it dawned on me that not only does God care for me but He has also intentioned my life toward His purposes. He has a plan and I am a part of it! I wrote about God's intention in a book called *Extraordinary Living*. The premise of the book was that we have an extraordinary God who gives ordinary people extraordinary lives.

Then one day a couple of years ago, some co-workers and I had a discussion about the Christian life and we found that we agreed that there are specific ways in which Christ followers are continually developing, and these ways prepare them for God's purposes in this world. That discussion led us on a journey of discovery.

The journey led us to read, study, discuss, and invite interested and knowledgeable people to think and pray with us. Our personal experience, along with the input of scholars, practitioners, and other believers, led us to seven foundational areas of growth that equip us for God's purposes in this world. In *Intentional Living* you will find these seven areas, or intentions, described and applied. In no way is this book intended as a comprehensive, flawless summary of these seven areas, but rather as a reflection of specific ways God has spoken to me concerning His purposes. As you read these intentions, it is my hope that you will want to explore these areas for yourself and begin an intentional journey of growth in all of them.

Intentional living is a lifetime journey of discovery with God. Choosing to live for God's purposes requires a commitment to His mission, or what is called a *missional life*. In other words, intentional living is choosing to commit to God's mission to restore mankind to a relationship with Him. What does it mean to have a missional spirituality? A missional understanding of the Scriptures? A missional worldview? Missional relationships? Missional communication? A missional ministry? A missional leadership? Many answers to these questions will be unique for each of us, but they all require an intentional commitment.

More than 25 years ago I felt God's admonition to join Him in His mission. He opened my heart not only to the community in which I lived but also to a whole world that needs to know Jesus Christ. He intentioned me for His mission, right where I live and to the ends of the earth, even the places I may never go.

In this journey I have found that not only did God intention something for my life but He has also called me to an intentional response. Intentional living is the only right response to a loving God who has already initiated His intentions for us.

CHAPTER ONE

LIVING INTENTIONALLY for God

For Christians, God alone sets the agenda.
—Henry and Richard Blackaby, *Spiritual Leadership*

HE WAS A TOP EXECUTIVE at one of America's leading companies, and he sat next to me on my flight to Dallas. We began to chat, and our conversation led us into a discussion of life. Suddenly, he hesitated, turned to look at me, and said, "I have power and wealth. I have a beautiful wife, wonderful children, and the position and success envied by many. I have achieved everything I set out in life to do, but I am empty on the inside. I have it all, but it isn't enough." He had followed his own plan and discovered it led nowhere.

Shortly after this, I was watching my youngest grandson, Nicolas, put a wooden puzzle of animal shapes together. He was intent on making a lion-shaped puzzle piece fit into a chicken-shaped hole. Needless to say, it wouldn't go in. In fact, it wasn't until I took his hand and guided it toward the lion-shaped hole that Nicolas was able to put the puzzle together. I couldn't help but think of the executive on the airplane. Like so many of us, he had taken the puzzle pieces of his life out of God's hands and he couldn't find where they fit.

> *God designed the puzzle we call life and He is the only one who can put the pieces together in a way that makes sense.*

God designed the puzzle we call life and He is the only one who can put the pieces together in a way that makes sense and is fulfilling to the very end. My father committed his life to Christ when I was in the eighth grade, and until the end of his life, what he gained in this intentional commitment to God outshone any worldly gain. I heard my father mention a number of times how much he wished he had made this commitment to God's plan earlier in life.

I've discovered God's plan is far better than any plan I come up with for myself. Just as Nicolas made a decision to let me guide his hand, I've made the decision to live according to God's plan rather than my own. It is a decision that brings value and purpose to every aspect of my life. It is an intentional commitment to God and His purposes. Every moment lived apart from God's plan is a wasted opportunity to move from emptiness to fullness, from brokenness to wholeness, from meaninglessness to purposeful living.

When was the last time you made an intentional decision for God in your life? Have you moved through life unintentionally? Have you found yourself in a place in life you never thought you would be? God has a perfect, purposeful plan for your life. Are you ready to live for God's purposes? I invite you to intentional living.

What Is Intentional Living?

Intentional living is a decision. It is the one decision that will guide your life toward God—God's purposes and God's plan for you. It is the decision that will ensure a life well lived, a life that matters, a life that makes a difference in the world. It is a committed, daily choice to live for God's purposes—not your own purposes, not your parents' or your spouse's, but God's purposes. It is not living accidentally, or by luck, but by choice. Intentional living is all about choosing to live for God and His purposes alone.

The word *intentional* describes the process of your life. Rather than leaving the way you live to chance, you make a commitment to the kind of life that pleases God and to the things in this world that matter to God. The word *living* refers to the daily act of staying true to your commitment. Intentional living is to live for God's purposes, or God's plan, or God's mission. In other words, to live intentionally is to live *missionally*—that is, for God's mission.

History tells the story of people who lived intentionally for God's mission. You may know that the Red Cross was started by a nurse named Clara Barton who chose to put her life in harm's way to bring healing to those on the front lines of the Civil War. The Salvation Army started with a man named William Booth who planted his life among the homeless and hungry in London. Francis of Assisi left a life of privilege to follow God, and his actions resulted in thousands taking up the way of sacrifice and service as Franciscan monks. John Bunyan wrote *The Pilgrim's Progress* while imprisoned for refusing to quit preaching the gospel. None of these individuals knew at the time that their deliberate choice to live only for God's mission would result in the transformation of lives for generations to come.

Each and every day, ordinary people become extraordinary people as they choose to let God's mission be their own, as they make an intentional decision to live for God's purposes alone. Throughout this book you will meet friends of mine whose intentional lifestyle is all about God and the things in this world that concern Him. They understand that they are intentioned for God's mission.

Are you living for God's mission? Are you intentionally committing your life to God's purposes? There is something wonderful about having the best seat in the house, or a seat on the 50-yard line. Living intentionally for God's mission gives you not only the best view of life but brings you closer to the God who knows exactly what your life should be. Why would you choose any other way of living when you are invited by God Himself to journey with Him into His purposes His way?

INTENTIONED FOR GOD'S MISSION

Henry and Richard Blackaby write in their book *Spiritual Leadership*, "People are looking for someone to lead them into God's purposes God's way." Jesus made it clear that Christians, whatever their chosen vocation and life commitment, have been intentioned for God's purposes. In His prayer found in John 17, Jesus affirms the intention of God for His children.

> *I am not asking you to take them out of the world, but I ask you to protect them from the evil one. They do not belong to the world, just as I do not belong to the world. Sanctify them in the truth; your word is truth. As you have sent me into the world, so I have sent them into the world.*
>
> —John 17:15–18

In these few words, we see that our lives are intentioned toward a purpose. Jesus told His followers that He was leaving and they could not go with Him. He had spent hours and hours, day after day, preparing them for the day when He would leave them. Why did Jesus not ask God to take us out of the world? Simply because God wants us to stay engaged in what He is doing here on earth. He sent us into the world, just as Jesus had been sent into the world.

Since this is so, *why we live, how we live,* and *where we live* are important questions we need to ask ourselves if we are to live intentionally for God's purposes.

WHY WE LIVE

Perhaps the most revealing question is *Why do you live?* Joshua declared:

> *Now if you are unwilling to serve the Lord, choose this day whom you will serve, whether the gods your ancestors served in the region beyond the River or the gods of the Amorites in whose land you are living; but as for me and my household, we will serve the Lord.*
>
> —Joshua 24:15

Paul wrote to the Christians in Corinth, "So whether we are at home or away, we make it our aim to please him" (2 Corinthians 5:9). My granddaughter called me one night when she was nine years old. "Grandmommy, I have something to tell you," she said. "What is it, Chelsea?" I asked. "Grandmommy, I became a Christian tonight." Chelsea made the intentional decision for why she would live.

Have you made this decision? Paul and Silas, two missionaries in the Bible, were thrown in prison. When they were miraculously released, the jailer cried out, "Sirs, what must I do to be saved?" Paul and Silas answered, "Believe on the Lord Jesus, and you will be saved, you and your household." The jailer and all of his family made the decision for why they lived. We are never too old to make an intentional decision for why we live.

The why of life is settled when we commit our lives to God in His Son Jesus Christ. At that moment we become new people with a new reason for living. We are freed from the death of sinfulness to a new life of forgiveness!

> *And when you were dead in trespasses and the uncircumcision of your flesh, God made you alive together with him, when he forgave us all our trespasses, erasing the record that stood against us with its legal demands. He set this aside, nailing it to the cross.*
>
> —Colossians 2:13–14

From the moment we awaken to the sacrifice of Christ for us, God begins to work in our hearts to reveal His character and will to us and through us. In a sense, we choose the why of life every day as we choose to obey God and become more like Christ.

The Apostle Paul wrote letters to Christians living in Corinth, Ephesus, Galatia, Rome, Philippi, Colossae, and Thessalonica. In each of these letters he encouraged believers to let go of their human way of thinking and "lead a life worthy of the calling to which you have been called" (Ephesians 4:1). Because God has given us a free will and sealed us to Himself by giving each of us the presence of the Holy Spirit, every decision we make is an opportunity to affirm again and again the why of our lives. It is not until we know why we live that we can begin to consider how we live.

How We Live

When did you decide how to live? From the time my grandchildren were born, their mother, my daughter, has been intentional in shaping their values. She has guided them in deciding what they would watch and read, where they would go for school and for fun, and with whom they would play. She has taken them to church, studied the Bible with them, and encouraged them to learn and develop their areas of interest and ability. Recently, she and my granddaughter joined the orchestra at their church, not only to participate in the worship experience but to provide accountability for use of their musical skills in flute and violin.

It is not until we know why we live that we can begin to consider how we live.

Paul was deeply concerned with how people live, so much so that he was a concerted pray-er for this very need. One of his prayers is recorded in Colossians 1:9–14. *The Message* paraphrase puts Paul's prayer in clear and simple terms.

> *Be assured that from the first day we heard of you, we haven't stopped praying for you, asking God to give you wise minds and spirits attuned to his will, and so acquire a thorough understanding of the ways in which God works. We pray that you'll live well for the Master, making him proud of you as you work hard in his orchard. As you learn more and more how God works, you will learn how to do your work. We pray that you'll have the strength to stick it out over the long haul—not the grim strength of gritting your teeth but the glory-strength God gives. It is strength that endures the*

unendurable and spills over into joy, thanking the
Father who makes us strong enough to take part in
everything bright and beautiful that he has for us. God
rescued us from dead-end alleys and dark dungeons. He's
set us up in the kingdom of the Son he loves so much, the
Son who got us out of the pit we were in, got rid of the
sins we were doomed to keep repeating.

The decision for how to live has tremendous implications. When my friend Laura was teaching in a Romanian university, she was asked to change a grade for the daughter of the university president. When she refused, she lost her position. Staying true to her values came at a high price, but it was a price she was willing to risk.

An intentional decision regarding how we live will affect our responses to the situations that come our way. And how we respond to each situation will impact our relationship to God, our view of the world, our character, our relationships, our vocation—every aspect of who and what we become, even where we choose to live.

WHERE WE LIVE

How did you decide where to live? Perhaps you've stayed in one community for your entire life, or you've lived all over the world. According to Ray Bakke, founder of International Urban Associates, where we live must be an intentional decision, based on God's plan rather than our own. In his book *A Theology as Big as the City*, Bakke asks, "Does God care only about people, or does he also care about places, including cities?" God cares about places. Scripture identifies specific places as much as it identifies specific people. And when those places are mentioned, we discover that God is very aware of the people who live there, including every need they face, whether it is physical, social, or spiritual. Scripture often allows us to hear from God's own heart regarding His anguish over the mistreatment or the spiritual condition of the people. God cares about places.

A close look at Scripture reveals God's active involvement in where people live. Think for a moment about a few of the places and the decisions of God related to these places that we find in Scripture. God intentionally moved Abraham from one place to another to fulfill God's future plan for the coming Savior. The Lord intentionally put Joseph in prison in Egypt to see the Hebrew people through a terrible famine. God sent Moses to Egypt to free the Israelites. The Lord brought the Israelites to the Promised Land. In fact, He also gave the Israelites the route they were to take with their moving vans! Daniel was taken captive so God could use him in Babylon. Jonah was sent to Nineveh and tried to get away from God by going to Tarshish. (You may remember that this didn't work!) Jesus' parents were guided by the Lord to live for a time in Bethlehem, Egypt, and Nazareth. Where they lived mattered because it involved their protection and the fulfillment of prophesies that the Savior would be born in Bethlehem and yet be called a Nazarene.

Most of us choose our place to live based on comfort, location, safety, school systems, retirement plans, extended family . . . and the list goes on. Most of us, if we can afford it, and if we are free to do it, flee from the places where life is not easy. We do not want to live where poverty is visible, crime is high, and beauty is not evident. Scripture does not give weight to these approaches regarding where we live. Consider how often the Lord sent His people away from family, away from security, away from luxury, and to the places where people needed a word from the Lord.

Have you noticed how often church members vote to

move the location of their meeting place when the community begins to change, when the "neighbors" aren't like them anymore, or the homes begin to transition into ghettos? Ray Bakke suggests that such decisions may seem simply practical; but, in fact, they are theological. God cares where we live and where our churches meet.

Where God would have us live can change from one season of our lives to another. I've lived in many places, but I know others whom God has called to live in the same city for their entire lives. Where we live is all about being in the place where God would have us accomplish His mission. You don't have to go far to discover people who have a need. Whether you live on a rural, tree-lined street, in a downtown high-rise condo, or high in the mountains, people around you have needs. You have the opportunity to be intentional in whatever way God has gifted you to show His love to those in need.

> *Intentional living is an act of worship influencing every part of life.*

Why we live, how we live, and where we live are intentional decisions for those who choose God's purposes as their own. When all aspects of our life take shape in an intentional process, we see God lifted up. Intentional living is an act of worship influencing every part of life.

AN EXAMPLE OF INTENTIONAL LIVING

Perhaps you are wondering what a life might look like when lived intentionally toward God's purposes. The creativity of God as He fulfills His plan through people is endless, so no life can truly serve as a model for another because God's working in each life will be different. But from time to time I encounter an individual or a family in whom I see unusual commitment to intentional living.

Ray Bakke is the founder of International Urban

Associates and has worked in inner-city ministry since 1959; his life underscores what it means to be intentional in living for God's purposes. Years ago he moved to the inner city of Chicago from Washington State to plant a church and raise his children in a low-income, inner-city community. He invested his life in the issues of poverty, crime, and violence, which plagued this neighborhood. He saw God transform the entire community. It was this experience that prepared Ray Bakke to lead consultations in over 200 cities around the world to teach others how to transform their cities. Now he also teaches seminary students how to be transformational leaders.

A few years ago God led Ray and his wife, Corean, to return to Washington and build a home in the rural community where he grew up. The Bakkes have been as intentional in their move to this place as they were in their decision to live in Chicago. When they built their new home, their lifelong commitment to God's mission was carried over into its design and use. Until the end, they want to live *intentionally* for God's purposes. Each room is designed, and the property is landscaped, with their lifelong commitments in mind. I asked Corean to tell me the story behind its design. This story illustrates lifelong commitment to intentional living.

COREAN'S STORY

One day I asked my husband, "If we were to leave Chicago, where would you want to go?" When I asked the question, Chicago had been our home for over 20 years; it was where we had raised three sons, accumulated graduate degrees, pursued careers, and learned the art of urban living. Without hesitation Ray answered, "Saxon."

Saxon does not show on the map. It is a rural community adjacent to Acme, Washington, itself a village. My husband's great-grandfather homesteaded in Saxon. The farm is still owned and operated by the Bakke family.

On the eve of our flight to Seattle to visit the site, I wrote an eight-part theology for our future home: biblical, traditional, contextual, liturgical, sensual, artistic, pastoral, and joyful. Twelve years later I realize that all eight hopes are now present realities. Excerpts from my "Theology for Bakken" include:

Biblical—The architectural expression of biblical truth, for me, needs to express the truth of God through the honest use of solid materials. I try to avoid things which pretend to be something they are not.

Traditional—Connectedness with those who have gone before is important to me. . . . Our furniture will provide the link between the new and the old, the future and the past.

Contextual—I want to work with the terrain and the vegetation and the climate to find the kind of structure that seems to naturally suit this place and enhances the things already here.

Liturgical—We want to think carefully about our working needs so that our place will energize and enable our work to be the best offering we are capable of making.

Sensual—May this be a place where all the senses are invited to participate—where we pause to smell the flowers, where we delight in foods which satisfy our hunger, where our eyes feast on both natural and manmade surroundings, where our ears thrill with sounds of life, where our fingers and toes caress textures indoors and out.

Artistic—Just as God's creativity goes beyond function and becomes a work of art, we dream of this place as a unique piece of art in itself, as an eight-acre piece of sculpture.

Pastoral—We look forward to building a place where we will continue to share our lives and resources, where we pursue our calling to feed sheep and lambs.

Joyful—We want our home to be a place for concerts and art exhibitions, dancing and storytelling, conversation and laughter, nature walks and tractor rides, formal dinners and picnics.

Bakken (Norwegian for "the hill") has become a complex of tractor roads, numerous small buildings (a one-room cabin is the most significant), a grotto, an open-air chapel, picnic tables, and trails. My husband spent an entire winter back in Chicago selecting 20 people, 1 from each century since Christ, whose missions efforts made a significant difference in the history of the church. He has 20 markers on a 2,000-foot trail and a little book with a page to read at each marker. Hundreds of people have walked the missions trail.

When we moved into the house we invited guests not for an open house but for a piano recital in a diamond-shaped room overlooking the valley and adjoining mountains. We have used that room for banquets, board meetings, and faculty retreats. When our numbers are few, we congregate in the kitchen in front of a fireplace made of stones from the river where my husband played as a boy, or in his library upstairs.

Our home and grounds are an awesome responsibility. My husband and I consider ourselves stewards of Bakken. Daily we acknowledge our gratitude and pray for continued guidance for our lives and work.

~

The Journey to Intentional Living

How long has it been since you made an intentional decision that shaped your life? We have no better time than right now to begin living intentionally for God and His mission. Jesus said of Himself:

> *The Spirit of the Lord is upon me, because he has anointed me to bring good news to the poor. He has sent me to proclaim release to the captives and recovery of sight to the blind, to let the oppressed go free, to proclaim the year of the Lord's favor.*
>
> —Luke 4:18–19

Then He said, "Today this scripture has been fulfilled in your hearing" (Luke 4:21). Now is the time to begin living intentionally for God and His mission. So how can we do this? How can we become intentional in preparing ourselves for God's purposes, for God's mission in this world?

This morning, as I stood with my church choir before we entered the sanctuary, I realized that my mind was on many things other than the reason I had come to church this Sunday morning. It was driven home to me that God expected me to be intentional about my faith, including my involvement in worship on Sunday morning. I wasn't there to accidentally hear from God. I was there to present my heart, soul, mind, and strength to God in worship of Him. Jesus said the greatest commandment is this:

> *The first is, "Hear, O Israel: the Lord our God, the Lord is one; you shall love the Lord your God with all*

your heart, and with all your soul, and with all your mind, and with all your strength. The second is this, "You shall love your neighbor as yourself." There is no other commandment greater than these.

—Mark 12:29–31

Intentional living begins by loving God with heart, soul, mind, and strength. Jesus' command infers that God expects us to show up each day with our entire being ready to join Him in what He is doing in our lives and in the entire world.

You may not be able to plan for the future, but you can prepare. Begin by loving God with your whole being. Intentionally commit to think with God's mind, see through God's eyes, embrace God's personality, feel with God's heart, tell God's story, influence with God's light, and serve with God's strength. As you journey through the following chapters, explore and evaluate your intentional commitment to live for God and His purposes only.

Review your plan for the future. Do you have one? Where does God fit in?

CHAPTER TWO

INTENTIONAL PREPARATION

The future belongs to those who prepare for it, not those who plan for it.

—Reggie McNeal, *The Present Future*

VONETTA FLOWERS, THE FIRST PERSON of African descent to win a gold medal in the Winter Olympic Games, dreamed of winning an Olympic gold medal as a track star from the time she was nine years old. That dream led her to an intentional decision to prepare herself as an athlete. When injuries closed the door to track and field for her in 2000, another door unexpectedly opened in the winter sport of bobsled. But then the new dream of going to the Olympics as a bobsledder seemed as if it too were going to be dashed when Vonetta was suddenly cut from her team only a few months before the 2002 Winter Games.

In her book *Running on Ice,* Vonetta explains that it was faith—both her own and her husband Johnny's—that kept her going. "I kept training. . . . I believed that God really did put me in this sport for a reason. . . . I had no idea what would happen, but, in faith, I continued working on my sport. As I look back, I could have never foreseen what would happen in the days ahead. It was nothing short of remarkable." Two weeks later, she had not one, but two offers to join the bobsled team. Vonetta's success has allowed her to speak of her faith in forums that would not be open to her if she had been unequipped for the coming challenge of the US bobsled team. Her obedience to God and her continual preparation opened doors she could not anticipate.

> *God has the plan, knows the plan, and is working the plan.*

INTENTIONAL PREPARATION

Reggie McNeal, in his book *The Present Future,* writes that while we cannot plan for the future, we can prepare. God has the plan, knows the plan, and is working the plan. Jeremiah 29:11 gives assurance of this: "For surely I know the plans I have for you, says the LORD, plans for your welfare and not for harm, to give you a future with hope." God makes it clear that He has the plan. We may know part of the plan; we may even have an intentional goal for our lives, like Vonetta Flowers did for the Olympics. But like Vonetta, we may discover that God's plan is slightly, or even significantly, different from our own.

Even so, we can prepare. In the weekly Bible study that I have with my teenaged granddaughter, we read together the story Jesus told of the ten bridesmaids, five of whom prepared for the coming of the bridegroom, and five who were not ready. While they all knew that the bridegroom was coming, they did not know when. Five were wise and kept their lamps filled with oil, ready to go. The others missed his coming when their lamps began to go out.

Jesus told His followers, "'It is not for you to know the times or periods that the Father has set by his own authority. But you will receive power when the Holy Spirit has come upon you; and you will be my witnesses in Jerusalem, in all Judea and Samaria, and to the ends of the earth'" (Acts 1:7–8). Jesus gave us God's plan but confirmed that we will not know the details of how, when, and where. Rather, He wants us to live in such a way that we are equipped and ready for whatever lies ahead. Would Vonetta have been asked to join the bobsled team if she had not already proven to be fast and strong because of her athletic preparation? Vonetta did not know exactly what opportunities the future would bring. Yet her intentional approach to life prepared her for what lay ahead, as God's agenda was made known to her.

Prepared by God for Intentional Living

God's agenda is where preparation begins. As we open ourselves to His leading, He guides us in ways that allow Him to prepare us for His plan. He is not only beside us, but also before us.

Think back again to Jesus' prayer in John 17:15–18. In these few words we begin to see how God prepares us for His mission.

I am not asking you to take them out of the world, but I ask you to protect them from the evil one. They do not belong to the world, just as I do not belong to the world.

Sanctify them in the truth; your word is truth. As you have sent me into the world, so I have sent them into the world.

1. God intentionally protects us. "I ask you to protect them from the evil one." Jesus' first request was that God would protect us from the evil one. God Himself is protecting us while we are here. We are not in the world alone. Rather, God is here with us. We can know that there is indeed *divine* intervention, *divine* involvement, and *divine* outcomes for our lives. As Jesus prepared to leave the world, He was intensely aware that we would face temptations and sorrows as "the evil one" seeks to wreak havoc upon our lives. He determined far in advance that we would have divine help and protection. Again and again, Jesus gave assurance that when He left, the Holy Spirit would come to us, bringing into our lives wisdom, strength, and power to defeat the enemy.

The need for protection is a clear message that life is going to be tough. Obviously, our human resources do not provide all that we need to survive in this world. Whatever lies ahead will call for a divine presence and initiative that we cannot provide in our own power. Jesus' prayer reminds us that we need God. We need Him every day in every situation.

What does it mean that we have divine protection? When we listen to the news and hear of persecution, suffering, and injustice toward those who believe, it seems that the Protector may not be doing His job. Yet, God promises this to His children:

The Lord is your keeper; the Lord is your shade at your right hand. The sun shall not strike you by day, nor the moon by night. The Lord will keep you from all evil; he

*will keep your life. The Lord will keep your going out
and your coming in from this time on and forevermore.*

Even though we may not understand the circumstances,
God tells us that we are never out of His hands; nothing
ever "unintentionally" happens to us when God is in control. God promised to protect us, and Jesus prayed for our
protection. Even homeland security cannot promise the
protection that God can give!

A Story of Intentional Protection

Harvey Thomas, who served as public relations coordina-
tor for Margaret Thatcher, former prime minister of Great
Britain, discovered how God is in control when an IRA
bomb exploded in a London hotel where he was staying,
along with Prime Minister Thatcher and others in her
staff. The bomb demolished four levels of the hotel and
killed five of Thomas's closest friends. Harvey Thomas
was angry, and remained that way for almost eight years.
The turning point came when he attended a conference
on reconciliation. After consulting his wife, Harvey
Thomas wrote to the hotel bomber, who had since been
caught and imprisoned. The bomber's name was Patrick
Magee.

Thomas wrote Magee in prison and revealed his identity. In the letter, he forgave Magee because of Christ's
forgiveness. Once he forgave Magee, he immediately felt
free of the anger he had carried for years. When Magee
was released from prison, Thomas wrote him again and
asked to meet him; he hoped to lead Magee to Christ.
Thomas invited Magee to England and sent him an airline
ticket to London. When Thomas picked him up, he
decided to take Magee home for breakfast. Patrick Magee

was amazed at how Harvey and his family welcomed him into their home, even after the actions he had taken against them. Harvey Thomas and his family now call Patrick Magee a friend and have ministered to him as they have shown love and forgiveness that could only be attained through divine power.

Jesus' prayer, "I ask you to protect them from the evil one," was answered in Harvey Thomas's life! What was intended by man as evil, God intended for good toward Patrick Magee. The anger that evil had caused in Harvey Thomas's own heart gave way to a testimony of God's power to free us from hatred and fill us with love.

2. God intentioned that we belong to Him. "They do not belong to the world." The world has its own agenda. Jesus placed us in a unique group—He put us in *His* group! What a compliment to us. We belong to God! We are His children, and He is a Father who will never leave us, and never disappoint us. The Apostle John wrote:

> *But to all who received him, who believed in his name, he gave power to become children of God, who were born, not of blood or of the will of the flesh or of the will of man, but of God.*

> —John 1:12

Do you have any idea how many people in this world are looking for a father who will not leave them or disappoint them? One of the saddest realities of our world is of fathers who have abused and abandoned their families. The tragic result of this abandonment is that there are hundreds of young men entering adulthood without a loving father's example to follow, and there are thousands of young women looking for the love they never received from a father.

Maybe you are one of these men or women. Maybe you need to know that in Christ you can belong to the most loving, gracious Father in the universe, a Father who is always present and actively concerned with your every need. Jesus spoke of God in the most intimate terms, calling Him *Abba*, the same as Daddy in contemporary English. Jesus is the one who removed the barrier that separates us from the divine God so that we might call Him *Abba*.

Belonging to God, our Abba, rather than the world, means we have access to unconditional love and acceptance. He doesn't choose us based on our beauty, money, education, popularity, or success. He makes us His children because He loves us, and there is no better way for Him to show His love than to "adopt" us into His family and His care. He takes us out of the world and brings us into His love. He guides us into fulfilling daily relationships and meaningful work. He gives us the Holy Spirit to remind us every day that He is guiding us toward a day of completion, that He is there with us, blessing us, loving us, forgiving us, and fulfilling all His promises to us. Our Abba goes with us into every circumstance and every situation. He molds our desires in ways that allow Him to fulfill our heart's cry for Him. His love embraces us, whatever we do, wherever we go, for all our years, throughout eternity. You have been intentionally set apart for God. God has intentioned that you look to Him as a Father, your Abba. An intentional approach to life recognizes God as Father and seeks His leading in all aspects of life.

God has intentioned that you look to Him as a Father, your Abba.

If someone were observing your life today, to whom would they think you belong? Perhaps they would immediately say, "You seem to have something that is uniquely different. What is it?" If this is the case, then you must be living intentionally for God's mission.

3. God intentioned that we be set apart for His mission. "Sanctify them in the truth; your word is truth." When John uses the word *sanctify*, it is always toward a mission. In other words, we are set apart as God reveals Himself and His will through the Holy Spirit, and we commit our lives to God's will. The Holy Spirit teaches us about God—His heart, His will, and His plan. Truth is what sets us apart, and we then make His will our deliberate choice for life.

The world does not live by truth. The dividing line is found at this point. Our being sanctified or set apart comes entirely from our response to God's truth, not from who we are. *The Message* gives us this interpretation of Ephesians 1:13:

> *It's in Christ that you, once you heard the truth and believed it (this Message of your salvation), found yourselves home free—signed, sealed, and delivered by the Holy Spirit.*

Truth is powerful. In his book *Christian Theology*, Millard J. Erickson explains, "Truth generates from above, from a higher source. It is God who speaks and man who is on trial, not the other way around." Truth is in opposition to human standards for belief and behavior. Isn't this why the courts for many years required witnesses to make an oath of truth with their hand placed on a Bible? A high-profile trial involved Scott Peterson, accused of killing his wife and unborn child. At first glance, he looked the perfect husband. But within days, his infidelity, selfishness, and lies revealed a man completely unknown to his friends and family. His life proved to be empty of truth and packed with deceit. As the trial unfolded, more and more evidence of his hidden side was exposed. His conviction became nearly self-evident by the end of the trial, when anyone watching could see little reason to believe anything he had said in his defense. While Peterson seems an extreme case, he is illustrative of humankind apart from the truth of God. There is no real truth except as is found in Christ, for Christ is Truth. Jesus said, "'I am the way, and the truth, and the life'" (John 14:6). Truth is evident only when seen through the lens of a relationship to God in Christ.

Jesus' prayer that we would be sanctified in truth is critical to understanding our lives. We cannot know the will of God apart from truth. The worst beliefs and behaviors may look good when seen through only our human understanding. Have you wondered how someone could murder another person? Or scam the savings of the elderly? Or abuse a child? Wonder no more! These are behaviors that come from minds and hearts leaning on their own understanding. These are lives lived apart from the intentionality of God's purposes.

The Apostle Paul was a fierce persecutor of Christians until he encountered Truth on the road to Damascus. His understanding of life was so transformed that he changed his name from Saul to Paul. He was horrified when he saw the way he lived, the way he thought, and the way he acted through the lens of Truth. But he wasn't just shamed by looking back; he was also filled with hope as he looked forward. For the first time, he began to understand who he was and what he was to be doing on this earth. For the first time, life made sense. And so it was that from that time forward he spoke the truth in Christ.

I am speaking the truth in Christ—I am not lying; my conscience confirms it by the Holy Spirit—I have great

*sorrow and unceasing anguish in my heart. For I could
wish that I myself were accursed and cut off from
Christ for the sake of my own people, my kindred
according to the flesh. They are Israelites, and to them
belong the adoption, the glory, the covenants, the giving
of the law, the worship, and the promises; to them belong
the patriarchs, and from them, according to the flesh,
comes the Messiah, who is over all, God blessed forever.
Amen.*

—Romans 9:1–5

For the first time, Paul understood why God had sent him
into the world. For the first time Paul understood that He
was intentioned toward God's mission. From that time
forward Paul lived intentionally for God's mission alone.
Just as Jesus had been sent, so now he was being sent.

4. God intentionally sent us into the world. "I have
sent them into the world." The phrase "as you have sent
me into the world" provides a clue to what it means that
we are sent into the world. We are following in the steps
of Jesus. Just as He was sent, so now we are being sent.
Jesus has already walked where we are to walk. He has
already forded the rivers, built the bridges, and cleared the
pathways. We are Christ followers in a very real sense, for
we are following Jesus into the world where He has
already gone before. At least three important intentional
actions are evident in Jesus' life, death, and resurrection;
as followers of Christ, we must also seek to live out these
actions in the world.

a) Jesus came to point the way to God. From the day He
was old enough to "point," He aimed the hearts of people
toward God. The angel told Mary that Jesus would be
called "the Son of the Most High." Jesus confirmed His

relationship to God again and again. "But I do as the Father has commanded me, so that the world may know that I love the Father" (John 14:31). To see Jesus was to see God. To hear Jesus was to hear from God. Jesus is the perfect example of intentional living.

Other than Jesus, the Apostle Paul might be the most recognized person in the Bible who consistently lived for God's purposes and pointed people toward God. His intentional commitment to God's purposes allowed God to work in supernatural ways through his life. Whether Paul was on land or sea, in prison or free, he testified to "the God who made the world and everything in it, he who is Lord of heaven and earth, does not live in shrines made by human hands, nor is he served by human hands, as though he needed anything, since he himself gives to all mortals life and breath and all things" (Acts 17:24–25). Following the perfect model of Jesus and the example of Paul, how are you pointing the way to God in the world around you?

From the day He was old enough to "point," Jesus aimed the hearts of people toward God.

b) Jesus came to save. "Then Jesus said to him, 'Today salvation has come to this house, because he too is a son of Abraham. For the Son of Man came to seek out and to save the lost'" (Luke 19:9–10). One of my favorite stories is of Marinus Leonard LaRue, a merchant marine captain in the Korean War who evacuated 14,000 refugees from a North Korean port, transporting them on a ship designed to hold 60 people. In a desperate attempt to save their lives, Captain LaRue loaded all 14,000 on his ship and three days later delivered them safely to a new land. He was recognized for his determination to save as many lives as possible, regardless of the risk of his own life.

Yet the greatest hero of all is Jesus, who laid down His

life for every person willing to accept His sacrifice. The movie *The Passion of the Christ* was an effort to show the tremendous price paid by Christ for our sin. Jesus came to save, and we have been sent into the world to do the same thing. Paul wrote to the Christians in Corinth, "I have become all things to all people, that I might by all means save some. I do it all for the sake of the gospel, so that I may share in its blessings" (1Corinthians 9:22–23). Paul made an intentional decision to do everything he could possibly do to bring the lost to Christ. He was willing to suffer as well as give up his rights. Paul followed Jesus into the world and lived according to Jesus' example. Are you doing the same?

> Paul followed Jesus into the world and lived according to Jesus' example. Are you doing the same?

c) *Jesus came to serve.* He said to his followers, "Whoever wishes to be first among you must be slave of all. For the Son of Man came not to be served but to serve, and to give his life a ransom for many" (Mark 10:44–45). Do you know of any person who left a high-paying position to become someone's servant or slave? Probably not, but this is exactly what Jesus did. He gave up His throne in heaven to take up a towel and wash feet covered with dirt. He gave up the highest position in the universe to stoop to the lowest position on earth. His is a Cinderella story, but not a fairy tale. Jesus' example is a reality that we can count on. Cinderella was made a servant against her will, and then was rescued by the prince and regained her status. Jesus, on the other hand, willingly left heaven to become a servant, so He could once and for all be crowned King of kings and Lord of lords.

Servanthood is perhaps one of the great mysteries of living as a believer. The Bible shows us, and I have learned from my own experiences, that serving brings far greater joy than lordship. Yet I am perplexed that I find it so difficult to live as a servant. I still want to hang on to my power and prestige. Paul, when writing to the slaves of his day, wrote an admonition that is still valid today: "Whatever your task, put yourselves into it, as done for the Lord and not for your masters, since you know that from the Lord you will receive the inheritance as your reward; you serve the Lord Christ" (Colossians 3:23–24). Jesus came to serve us, and now it is our responsibility to follow Him in servanthood.

God's intention for us is revealed through the divine and human Jesus Christ. He waits for us to become intentional in following His example.

Prepared to Live for God

In *Intentional Living* we will look at seven intentions that God has for our lives as we seek to live as Christ followers. As you read through this book, you will see themes that appear again and again and, hopefully, with each encounter, the picture of what your life looks like when lived intentionally for God's mission will become more defined. You will begin to see your life not in black and white, but in the full spectrum of God's creative and redemptive plan.

How long has it been since you made an intentional decision that shaped your life? Did that decision draw you closer to God or lead you away from Him? Whatever your answer, intentional living will be unique for each believer who chooses to live out his or her passion for God. It is never too late to begin living intentionally for God and His mission.

Thank God for His intention for your life. Psalm 139:5 reads, "You hem me in, behind and before, and lay your hand upon me." Take time to let God show you how His hand is guiding you intentionally toward the person He would have you be and the work He would have you do.

EMBRACING GOD'S CHARACTER:
Spirituality

*F*inally, be strong in the Lord and in the strength of his power. Put on the whole armor of God, so that you may be able to stand against the wiles of the devil. For our struggle is not against enemies of blood and flesh, but against the rulers, against the authorities, against the cosmic powers of this present darkness, against the spiritual forces of evil in the heavenly places. Therefore take up the whole armor of God, so that you may be able to withstand on that evil day, and having done everything, to stand firm. Stand therefore, and fasten the belt of truth around your waist, and put on the breastplate of righteousness. As shoes for your feet put on whatever will make you ready to proclaim the gospel of peace. With all of these, take the shield of faith, with which you will be able to quench all the flaming arrows of the evil one. Take the helmet of salvation, and the sword of the Spirit, which is the word of God.

—*Ephesians 6:10–17*

EMBRACING GOD'S CHARACTER

Empowered living involves the act of falling down before the highest power, the Holy Spirit.

—Esther Burroughs, *Empowered*

I will never forget the evening my neighbor said to me, "How can I see God?" When she said that, my prayer was, "Lord, may I live in such as way that she will see You in me."

We have great potential when we embrace God's character. He is the only thing we need to move from ordinary to extraordinary, from powerless to powerful. He lifts us from the limitations of our humanity to experience His divine initiative. He completes our personalities with His character and we experience wholeness. We become "imitators of God, as beloved children" (Ephesians 5:1). Becoming like God is not a suggestion, but a requirement of the Christian life.

> *Becoming like God is not a suggestion, but a requirement of the Christian life.*

This requirement at first seems beyond human ability. How can we possibly become like God? In fact, how can we even begin to know who God is and what His character is like? The fact is, we don't have to look far. Jesus was a perfect representation of His Father, God. When we know Jesus, we know God. The Apostle Paul wrote to the Christians in Philippi, "Let this same mind be in you that was in Christ Jesus, who, though he was in the form of God, did not regard equality with God as something to be exploited, but emptied himself, taking the form of a slave, being born in human likeness. And being found in human form, he humbled himself and became obedient to the point of death—even death on a cross" (Philippians 2:5–8). In other words, we are to be like Christ. In Christ we see

God, Creator of the universe, who became the sacrificial Lamb. While God is more than we can comprehend, we are called to assume His likeness so that we might represent Him to the world.

Taking on God's character in this way can never happen accidentally. It can only happen when we make it the intention of our lives. Scripture assures us that God has given us a helper for this very purpose. He has given us His Holy Spirit.

> *It's in Christ that you, once you heard the truth and believed it (this Message of your salvation), found yourselves home free—signed, sealed, and delivered by the Holy Spirit. This signet from God is the first installment on what's coming, a reminder that we'll get everything God has planned for us, a praising and glorious life.*
>
> —Ephesians 1:13–14 (*The Message*)

We have the Holy Spirit. The more we open our lives to His teaching, the more we are able to represent our God. The Spirit leads us into disciplines through which God reveals Himself—prayer, Bible study, and obedience. God reveals Himself through these common practices so that we will be more like Him.

My friend Edna Ellison is a woman who practices prayer, Bible study, and obedience. Her commitment to prayer and Scripture study is evident in the way she lives. When I asked her to tell me about a spiritual discipline that had been important in her fulfillment of God's mission, she immediately told me, "Obedience." Then she told me of a significant event that started her on the intentional journey of obedience to God's mission. Here is Edna's story.

~

EDNA'S STORY

My life changed dramatically one Friday night. I went to a championship football game a happily married wife and mother, and I came home a widow. My husband had slumped in the stadium seat and died of a massive heart attack. Two years later I accepted a marriage proposal. I thought the grief and loss would be behind me, but the engagement ended in a broken relationship. Two weeks after my fiancé asked for his ring back, I promised to speak before 200 women at a local YMCA. I casually opened my Bible that week, expecting the usual devotional outline to fall into place. Strangely, the verses in Philippians 4, which usually came alive as I studied them, lay flat on the page, saying nothing to my waiting heart. Holding up my Bible, I prayed, "Lord, anoint Your words on these pages, and anoint me to share them."

Nothing. I felt desperate.

"O Lord," I prayed again, "Please give me something to say."

Again nothing.

I prayed all week, and on the last afternoon, I begged: "Lord, I've got nothing to say tonight. Please speak through me. I beg You—anoint me; anoint Your Word." I turned the pages of my Bible, searching. It fell open at Isaiah 61:1—"The LORD has anointed me."

That caught my attention. I read on, as these words seemed to jump off the page: "The LORD has anointed me . . . to bind up the brokenhearted."

"I like to talk about joy," I said. "I know nothing about brokenness." Confronting me, God's Spirit seemed to say, *You know everything about brokenness. You've experienced the death of your husband—your best friend, your lover, your companion. Now you've had a broken engagement. Nothing is worse than love's rejection. You do know, from personal experience, about a broken heart.*

I didn't want to admit it, but after a few minutes' argument, I agreed. God demanded obedience from me, and—because I wanted to walk in the Spirit and not in the flesh—I was going to obey Him.

However, I wasn't happy about it. I obeyed with a grudge. I told the women about the brokenness of losing a husband in his 40s, about struggling as a single parent of teenagers, and finally about giving my heart in an engagement to someone who broke it. When I finished, I ran out of the banquet room and drove home. I remember looking up at God and saying aloud, "I hope You're satisfied. You've humiliated me, and what good did it do?"

The next day at school a fellow teacher, Kathy, told an unbelievable story. A night-school student, coming in tardy the night before, said she'd been rejected by her fiancé that afternoon. Returning his diamond symbolized her life, full of rejections, so she'd opted for suicide. After buying her nine-year-old son a membership to the YMCA, the last act of a dying mother, she heard the words, "If you are the most brokenhearted woman in the world, I have news for you. Jesus is the answer."

Following the voice, the young woman slipped into the back of the Y's banquet room, and, as she told Kathy later: "God saved me from suicide tonight. When I heard about that speaker's broken heart, I realized I was not alone. If God encouraged Edna, He could encourage me. I decided to stay alive, to go to all my boy's Y games! God also saved me for all eternity: I accepted Jesus as my Savior tonight. He's given me hope for the future!"

Through her story, God let me know my spiritual obedience was worthy in His sight. My walk with Him in the Spirit had allowed me to trust Him when times were hard, and—in a miraculous way— allowed me to share my faith with another who was hurting.

An Intentional Spirituality

This experience in Edna's life was transformational as she discovered more clearly who God is through her obedience. She was able to step out of herself to be His presence to a woman she did not know.

And so it is with us. A lifetime commitment to prayer, Bible study, and obedience leads us toward God's character. As we soak our lives in His presence, His love becomes our love. His compassion becomes our compassion. His view of life becomes our view. His message becomes our message. His mission becomes our mission. We abandon ourselves to God. We are the reflection of His goodness.

Abandoning ourselves to God's character is an intentional way of life. We choose to become like Him. We choose to become intentional in the lifetime disciplines that let us see Him—prayer, Bible study, and obedience.

Intentional About Prayer

Prayer is where you wage peace, joy, hope, and faith. Prayer is where your relationship to God becomes active and dynamic as you give Him access to your heart, the very place where His character becomes yours. Prayer is an all-day, everywhere connection to who God is. It's better than a cell phone, a wireless network, or a satellite signal. The divide that separates our humanity from God's divinity is bridged through prayer.

A friend of mine had a son who chose to join the cultic religion of his soon-to-be-new wife; my friend was discouraged, seeing no potential for a positive outcome. We both began to pray and listen for God's wisdom. As the marriage drew near, my friend experienced a deepened love and an assurance of God's ongoing work in her son's life. Several years have passed since then, and my friend and I have continued to marvel at God's ongoing work of redemption in her son's life.

THE RECONCILING POWER OF PRAYER

Only as we become like our Lord are we able to reconcile the issues of life with His will. Even Jesus, in His greatest hour of need, turned to God for the strength and peace He needed to face Gethsemane. He told His closest followers that He was grieved "even to death," and then He "threw himself on the ground and prayed that, if it were possible, the hour might pass from him. He said, 'Abba, Father, for you all things are possible; remove this cup from me; yet, not what I want, but what you want.'" Only as Jesus gave Himself completely over to who God is could He face the agony that was soon to come.

Jesus also knew that Peter, James, and John could not face the coming hours successfully unless they turned to God in prayer. He warned them to "keep awake and pray." He addressed this admonition directly at Peter, knowing that if Peter did not draw upon who God is through prayer, he would not have the resources within him to do God's will. The disappointment in Jesus' words when He returned from praying and found the disciples sleeping surely came from His knowledge that they would not have the spiritual resources to successfully face the coming trial. Sure enough, we know that Peter cut off the ear of a soldier and later denied knowing Jesus three times. The disciples ran away and hid. If Peter had chosen prayer over sleep, his actions in the hours before Christ's death might have been different. He needed God's strength and character.

When we pray, we turn from relying on our own human understanding to think with the mind of Christ.

When we pray, we turn from relying on our own human understanding and our own human strength to think with the mind of Christ and become imitators of God. Our response to life is according to who God is rather than who we are.

My friend Antoine Rutayisire witnessed the murder of his father by Hutus when he was five years old. "I was very angry because there was a long list of people I hated with cause." Antoine carried this hatred with him for years until he met Christ. He made a list of the offenders and asked God to help him forgive them. "When I finished that exercise, 20 years of hatred and bitterness were wiped out in one day." Eleven years later, the Hutu militia came to his front gate. His natural instincts were to protect his wife and children, to "go out and die like a man." But now he knew God's love and decided that he would not respond to their violence. He began to pray with his family. Almost miraculously, the Rwandan Patriotic Front rebels drove the militia away.

Only as we embrace who God is can we begin to be the ministers of reconciliation described by Paul in 2 Corinthians 5:17–21. As we become the righteousness of God, we can impact another life, another generation, and even the ultimate plan of God's redemption. The intentional decision to pray in all things and without ceasing is certainly a mission-critical commitment.

The Mission-Critical Role of Prayer

Praying is central to the fulfillment of God's purposes. Jesus set the example of praying without ceasing. For Jesus, prayer always preceded stepping out to engage God's plan.

Throughout the Old and the New Testaments we find numerous prayers recorded. Prayers were spoken for healing, safety, forgiveness, justice, and mercy, as well as for people and places. The Apostle Paul asked that his fellow believers pray for his personal boldness and safety. He included prayers in the letters he wrote and mentioned how often he prayed for the recipients of his letters.

The amazing truth about praying is that it is not a one-way discourse, but a conversation in which God reveals Himself to us. We embrace God's character as He speaks to us. The more we spend time in dialogue with Him, the more He reveals who He is and molds our desires and concerns to His desires and concerns. When God's character is brought to bear on life needs, things happen. Lives are changed. Societies are transformed. God's purposes are accomplished.

Intentional About Listening

Bringing God's character to bear on life requires a commitment to listen for God's voice. In a sense, when we listen we are surrendering ourselves to who God is. We are surrendering our will to God's will. In this way, God can then move us toward who He is in this world. I discovered this firsthand when taking Russian New Testaments into Moscow after the fall of Communism in the Union of Soviet Socialist Republics (USSR).

I was in the Moscow domestic airport, in line to have my passport checked. A large, stern military woman was checking the passports. When it came my turn, I heard the urging of the Spirit to give her the Russian New Testament that I had in my bag. But I didn't respond. I argued with the Spirit, refusing to hear God's voice. Just as I started to leave the room, a team member whispered in my ear, "Andrea, you should give that woman a Bible. You are the only one who has any left." God sent a messenger to tell me what He had already been saying to me. I was the vessel through whom He planned to show His love for this Russian woman.

> *Bringing God's character to bear on life requires a commitment to listen for God's voice.*

When my team member spoke to me, I knew I had to respond. So, with fear and trembling, I returned to the military woman, holding the New Testament for her to take. She accepted the book and began to read as people waited in line to have their passports checked. She looked at the book for at least five minutes, turning the pages as she read.

As I stood there, looking down where she was seated, I feared a tirade in Russian. But then she stood. With tears pouring down her cheeks, she said to me in Russian, "Thank you! Thank you! Thank you!" She raised her arms in the air and began to praise God for the Bible. She left the table where she sat and walked around the room, reading the Bible to every military person in the room. Her tears continued to fall, her praise was lifted high, and her face brightened with hope. She had been waiting all these years for God's Word to return to Russia, and now it had.

God wanted to love through me. God wanted to bring hope through me. Only when I listened could I become the reconciler He has called me to be. God wants us to know what is most important to Him and how He will accomplish His work through us. We aren't going to know until we listen.

Jesus listened to God and He often withdrew to pray. I believe that this was not only so He could talk to His Father, but also that He could *listen* to His Father. Surely Jesus sought to be in places where He could put all other voices aside. Jesus listened to God and responded to God's leading in every aspect of who He was and how He lived.

INTENTIONAL INTERCESSION

When we listen, we discover God's love for all people. Embracing God's character leads us to join God in redeeming people from sin, redeeming people from bondage, and all other issues that are at the heart of God's concern.

God's concern is evident in the story of His visit with Abraham on the way to destroy Sodom and Gomorrah. The Genesis account allows us to listen in on the Lord's thoughts as He decided to tell Abraham what He was about to do. Abraham responded by interceding for the peoples of Sodom and Gomorrah, finally asking the Lord to spare the cities if He found just ten righteous people. Not only did Abraham intercede, he waited and watched to see what happened. Scripture tells us that the Lord didn't find ten righteous people, but remembered Abraham and spared his nephew Lot, as well as Lot's family.

Just as the Lord came to Abraham, so the Lord comes to us. He comes to let us in on His heart. Can you imagine your name in the following Scripture passage? Every day the Lord is showing you who He is so you might respond according to who He is, so that you might become the intercessor for whom He is looking.

The Lord said, "Shall I hide from [your name] what I am about to do, seeing that [your name] shall become a

*great and mighty nation, and all the nations of the earth
shall be blessed in [him or her]? No, for I have chosen
[him or her], that [he or she] may charge [his or her]
children and [his or her] household after [him or her]
to keep the way of the Lord by doing righteousness and
justice; so that the Lord may bring about for [your
name] what he has promised [him or her]"*

—Genesis 18:17–19

Intercession is the work of God's people. Only those who
embrace His character have the privilege and accountability of intercession. Intercession isn't easy work. In fact, it
demands divine character, divine guidance, and divine per-
sistence. For Abraham, it meant coming back to God
again and again, as he sought to understand God's righteous and just activity. For Abraham, it included waiting
and watching to see what God would do. For Abraham, it
meant knowing God so well that he could trust Him with
the outcome.

INTENTIONAL BIBLE STUDY

Embracing God's character will lead us into Bible study.
Kenneth Taylor, founder of Tyndale House Publishers,
wrote *Living Letters*, what we now know as *The Living
Bible*, because of his deep concern that his children be
able to understand the Bible. When it comes to knowing
God, there is no other book so valuable and necessary to
our becoming like our namesake. Some people in our
world have memorized entire books of the Bible. Others
can find and quote verses by the hundreds. Wouldn't you
agree that a desire to become like God would cause us to
have a hunger for God's Word? So far I've found no other
written document than the Bible that shows me who God

is, that bridges the gap between the human and divine, that can free me from my human understanding, and that can lift me toward God and His purposes.

Contained within the pages of the Bible is God's character as He comes to us to comfort, strengthen, give wisdom, instruct, guide, admonish, convict, renew, save, and love. Written on every page is the story of God's purposes, carried down from one generation to another, to this very day, so that you and I might know God and His mission. Scripture is our guide for embracing God's character.

Scripture is our guide for embracing God's character.

SPIRITUAL HABITS FOUND IN SCRIPTURE

Embracing God's character leads to specific disciplines that further God's purposes. In their book *A Life That Matters*, Joanne Stuart Sloan and Cheryl Sloan Wray address several disciplines found in Scripture: prayer, meditation, fasting, Bible study, worship, praise, witnessing, service, stewardship, solitude, guidance, obedience, simplicity, and sacrifice. Each of these is a study in itself and reveals unique aspects of God's character and will.

For instance, not only does Scripture teach us much about simplicity, but many of the great Christian heroes of yesterday and today lived simply—Girolamo Savonarola, Augustine, Francis of Assisi, Blaise Pascal, Robert Barclay, Richard Baxter, and John Wesley, to name a few. I don't know about you, but I've discovered that the more I own, the more I have to worry with from day to day—bills to pay, upkeep to handle, and less time and money to engage the very things that God would have me be about.

Scripture also has much to say about sacrifice. When we think of sacrifice, our mind immediately turns to

Christ and His example. The Bible gives us many examples of sacrifice. A popular book that came out in the last few years is *Jesus Freaks*, which tells the stories of Christians who sacrificed their lives and liberty for Christ. Not long ago I walked through the slums of Delhi, India, with a friend who has planted his life there to meet spiritual and physical needs. Sacrifice is certainly a natural outcome of embracing God's character.

COMMUNITY

In an article in *Leadership Journal*, Henri Nouwen addressed three disciplines "by which we create space for God. It begins by being with God in solitude; then it creates a fellowship, a community of people with whom the mission is being lived; and finally this community goes out together to heal and to proclaim the good news" ("Moving from Solitude to Community to Ministry"). This progression of God's character in us can be traced through Scripture in the life and ministry of Jesus and Paul.

An often-missing component of contemporary American Christianity is hunger for community with fellow believers. Is it possible that we are not with God in solitude enough to hunger for time with other believers?

In his book *We Really Do Need Each Other*, Reuben Welch argues that it is only in community that God's character can enrich the lives of others. As divorce rates soar and families disintegrate, one contributing factor that has been identified is the lack of community. We are not together enough to trust one another with our deepest needs. Our fellowship never deepens beyond the Wednesday night meal and games on New Year's Day. We do not give or have the support we need to become more like Christ.

The discipline of community is one of the most winsome attributes of the Christian life to those who do not know Christ. The hunger to belong, to be loved unconditionally, is common to being created in God's image. As Nouwen explains, it is the community that goes out together to heal and proclaim the good news.

MISSIONS

The missions organization Woman's Missionary Union has identified six disciplines that should be found in the lives of all who embrace God's character. These are disciplines that bring the resources of God's people to bear on God's mission in the world.

Pray for missions: Talk to God about missions and intercede both for the missionaries and for the lost they are seeking to bring to the Lord. "At the same time pray for us as well that God will open to us a door for the word, that we may declare the mystery of Christ, for which I am in prison, so that I may reveal it clearly, as I should" (1 Colossians 4:3–4).

Give to missions: Provide financial support of missions work. "As it is written, 'He scatters abroad, he gives to the poor; his righteousness endures forever.' He who supplies seed to the sower and bread for food will supply and multiply your seed for sowing and increase the harvest of your righteousness" (2 Corinthians 9:9–10).

Do missions: Minister to people through redemptive, loving service in the name and spirit of Christ, and share the gospel with them. Doing missions is also witnessing to the gospel and giving another person the opportunity to confess Christ as Lord and Savior. "As you go, proclaim the good news, 'The kingdom of heaven has come near.' Cure the sick, raise the dead, cleanse the lepers, cast out demons" (Matthew 10:7–8).

Learn about missions: Be informed for better understanding and for responding sacrificially. "Then he opened their minds to understand the scriptures" (Luke 24:45).

Grow spiritually toward a missions lifestyle: Understand who God is and what He calls us to do in fulfilling the Great Commission. "Therefore be imitators of God, as beloved children, and live in love, as Christ loved us and gave himself up for us, a fragrant offering and sacrifice to God" (Ephesians 5:1–2).

Participate in the work of the church: God has established that it is through His church that His mission will be carried out. "All who believed were together and had all things in common; they would sell their possessions and goods and distribute the proceeds to all, as any had need" (Acts 2:44–45).

We embrace God's character with the goal that we will be "ambassadors for Christ, since God is making his appeal through us; we entreat you on behalf of Christ, be reconciled to God. For our sake he made him to be sin who knew no sin, so that in him we might become the righteousness of God" (2 Corinthians 5:20–21).

Transformed Through Scripture

Becoming the "righteousness of God" is transformation. God uses Scripture to teach, reprove, correct, and train us in righteousness (2 Timothy 3:16). The more we take time to learn from Him, the greater our transformation will be toward the character of God. We find assurance in Scripture that the Holy Spirit will be our helper to teach us all things, including the things of God that will transform our lives.

Calvin Miller tells in his book *The Unfinished Soul* of sitting in the Brussels Cathedral of St. Matthew and reading the second chapter of Acts as a cardinal led in the holiday mass. As Miller read, his heart and mind returned to the tent revival in Oklahoma where, 20 years earlier, he had committed his life to Christ. There in the cathedral, he discovered anew that the Spirit is doing the work of conversion, and "no matter the circumstance, the Spirit's coming is authentic, whenever and wherever it occurs."

The Apostle John explained in his letter that he was writing to ensure that his readers understood what they had in the anointing of the Holy Spirit in their lives.

As for you, the anointing that you received from him abides in you, and so you do not need anyone to teach you. But as his anointing teaches about all things, and is true and is not a lie, and just as it has taught you, abide in him.

—1 John 2:27

When we open our Bibles and allow the Holy Spirit to teach us, we discover anew God's love. We find in God's words the truth of who God is and what we can be when we embrace His character as our own. Every discipline for life is found in Him, recorded in Scripture, and interpreted for us through the Holy Spirit. Intentional living must include embracing God's character through prayer, Bible study, and obedience.

INTENTIONAL IN OBEDIENCE

Obedience is where we see God's character lived out through our lives. We discover what God can do when we give Him complete access to who we are and what we do. It ensures we will be in the right place at the right time with the right heart for God to accomplish His purposes through us. Jesus modeled obedience for us through His incarnation, perfectly embracing God's character.

And being found in human form, he humbled himself and became obedient to the point of death—even death on a cross.

—Philippians 2:8

Obedience leads to a sustaining faith as we discover again and again that God's character is sufficient for all our needs. God's character splashes out on those around us in actions of love, justice, and righteousness. We can't keep it from happening. When our hearts are filled with God's regard for others, their worth and success in life become a priority to us, and we become intentionally committed to God's purposes.

OBEDIENCE IS A TEST OF KNOWING GOD

Some years ago I introduced my granny to an acquaintance. This person immediately began to call Granny by this familiar term, even though I had introduced her by her given name. She said to me, "I'm not his granny!" In the same way, not everyone who calls on God's name truly knows Him. Consider for a minute these words from 1 John 2:3–4: "Now by this we may be sure that we know him, if we obey his commandments. Whoever says, 'I have come to know him,' but does not obey his commandments, is a liar, and in such a person the truth does not exist." Obedience is a test of knowing God. Those who know God have embraced His character to the extent that their lives are lived in obedience to His desires.

Those who know God have embraced His character to the extent that their lives are lived in obedience to His desires.

At the same time, obedience leads us to new desires. A friend of mine is experiencing God in ways she had not encountered Him before. I've seen her transformed as she has become more like God. As she embraces God's character, a whole new world of opportunity is becoming visible to her. Her desires have changed, resulting in a completely different view of what is important in life.

Jan David Hettinga explains in his book *Follow Me* that God calls us to obedience, but helps us to fulfill His commands. He helps us carry the burden of obedience that He assigns to us. Obedience is an invitation to work side by side with Him. Surely we could have no better partner in ministry than God Himself!

Obedience Is God's Character Revealed

Obedience is God's character lived out. It is the natural outcome of becoming like Him. We can't embrace God's character without desiring to live out who we have discovered God to be. If I applied for a position as an accountant, it wouldn't be long before my actions revealed that I know very little about accounting. In the same way, my actions reveal what I know about God.

Jesus said, "If I am not doing the works of my Father, then do not believe me" (John 10:37). He knew that His life was a complete reflection of His Father. There was no possibility that God would not be seen in His works. He knew His only desire was to please God.

God is the measure of our obedience. Obedience cannot come from a spirituality that leaves God out. Regardless of how good we may look to the world, God alone knows if our actions come from an intimate relationship with Him. Obedience, as with all good things, begins in God's heart and is extended to ours.

The reality of this is seen in the very fact of what it is that constrains us to give ourselves over to God's leadership. It is not our love for God, but rather God's love for us that leads us into obedience. Paul wrote to the church at Rome, "I appeal to you therefore, brothers and sisters, by the mercies of God, to present your bodies as a living sacrifice" (Romans 12:1). Paul understood that the motivation to unqualified obedience comes from God's mercies to us. Nothing else in life has the power to compel us to give God absolute sway over every thought, every word, every action that we take. This is the motivation that leads to the transformation of our minds, "so that you may discern what is the will of God—what is good and acceptable and perfect" (Romans 12:2).

In other words, obedience is a divine initiative that requires divine character and power. It is God working through us to accomplish His purposes in the world. It is God giving Himself away to us so that we might represent Him to those around us. It is the mercy of God lavished on us and through us. Obedience is the outcome of our intentional decision to embrace God's character, to respond to God's intention that we know Him and represent Him in the world. Our goal is that our lives and actions become exact representations of who God is, His character lived out through us. Embracing God's character is an intentional decision we make once and for all, renewed and lived out each day of our lives.

EMBRACING GOD'S CHARACTER

God wants us to know Him. "Thus says the LORD: 'Do not let the wise boast in their wisdom, do not let the mighty boast in their might, do not let the wealthy boast in their wealth; but let those who boast boast of this, that they understand and know me, that I am the LORD; I act with steadfast love, justice, and righteousness in the earth, for in these things I delight,' says the LORD" (Jeremiah 9:23–24).

Knowing God is a lifetime journey of prayer, Bible study, and obedience. When we know God, we also know what delights Him. He invites us to give our lives to this goal, to know God and to do what delights Him. Now we are beginning to see how we live intentionally toward God's mission. We begin with an intentional commitment to embrace God's character. Without this intention, God's purposes cannot be fulfilled through our lives.

Eric Liddell was a famous Scottish runner and a missionary to China (his story is told in the movie *Chariots of Fire*). Those who knew him when he was interned in Weihsien, a prison camp in the province of Shantung, North China, say that he stood out among the 1,800 people packed into the camp because he embraced God's character. His sacrifice, his service, his smile, his work and leadership—the list of what he gave and did for his fellow prisoners goes on and on—reflect his secret for living. Eric Liddell's two goals in life were to know God and make Him known to others.

Eric Liddell was *intentional* in choosing to live for God's purposes. Eric Liddell made an intentional commitment to embrace God's character as his own. This is a journey of intentional living that has as its destiny to know God and to make Him known.

Embracing God's Character

"What will we do with our lives? When God is the Infinite Center of them, we discover unequivocally that our purpose is 'to love God and serve him forever.' Our worship and adoration form us then to be Church in order to reach out to the world," says Marva Dawn in her book *A Royal "Waste" of Time*. Develop your plan today for intentional commitment to prayer, Bible study, and obedience, "God helping you: Take your everyday, ordinary life—your sleeping, eating, going-to-work and walking-around life—and place it before God as an offering" (Romans 12:1 *The Message*).

THINKING WITH GOD'S MIND:

Scripture Study

hen he opened their minds to understand the scriptures, and he said to them, "Thus it is written, that the Messiah is to suffer and to rise from the dead on the third day, and that repentance and forgiveness of sins is to be proclaimed in his name to all nations, beginning from Jerusalem. You are witnesses of these things. And see, I am sending upon you what my Father promised; so stay here in the city until you have been clothed with power from on high."

—Luke 24:45–49

Thinking with God's Mind

There must be, in any complete revelation of God's mind and will and character and being, things hard for the beginner to understand; and the wisest and best of us are but beginners.

—R. A. Torrey, *How to Study the Bible*

I happened upon an old journal in which I had written these words as a young woman: "I have begun an in-depth Bible study of *The Bible: God's Missionary Message to Man.*" Little did I realize then that this personal time spent in Bible study would transform my understanding of Scripture. I certainly did not understand how foundational this study would be for my own growth in intentional living. For the first time I saw the single thread of God's love for mankind weaving together the stories, the people, and the places mentioned throughout the Bible. I discovered God was stating His intention for mankind from the first verse of Genesis to the last verse of Revelation. For the first time, I began to understand how I fit into what God was doing. God had a plan and it included me. God *intentioned* my life toward His mission as described in His Word.

Since that time I have found that God's purposes are declared in beautiful ways, amazing stories, and ordinary people through whom God did extraordinary things. Scripture uses beautiful metaphors to describe "my part" of His purpose. Do you recall "the salt of the earth," "the light of the world," and "a city on a hill"? These are a few of the metaphors found in Scripture that describe God's missions plan for us. One of my favorites is "shine . . . like the stars forever and ever."

Songs in the Bible also declare God's purposes. Mary's song in Luke 1:46–55 is a celebration of God's promised Redeemer, as well as His provision and leadership traced from generation to generation and fulfilled in Jesus Christ. She sums up the working and planning of God in gracious words of praise. Elizabeth said of Mary, "Blessed is she who believed that there would be a fulfillment of what was spoken to her by the Lord" (Luke 1:45). Mary understood that she had been intentioned for God's purposes for all the nations.

> *As we understand God's mission for the world, we begin to see the world the way God sees it.*

The Apostle Paul described God's purpose when he wrote to the Christians in Ephesus. "This was in accordance with the eternal purpose that he has carried out in Christ Jesus our Lord, in whom we have access to God in boldness and confidence through faith in him" (Ephesians 3:11–12). Paul lived and breathed for the purposes of God. In every letter he wrote, he called God's people to God's mission. He understood Scripture to be about one thing, and that was God's love revealed in Jesus Christ, to be preached and taught to all people everywhere. He identified his part often. "I have become all things to all people, that I might by all means save some. I do it all for the sake of the gospel, so that I may share in its blessings" (1 Corinthians 9:22–23).

Intentional living is grounded in understanding the Bible as the missions book of God. As we understand God's mission for the world, we begin to see the world the way God sees it and we begin to understand what God is doing in the world; we begin to think with God's mind.

UNDERSTANDING GOD'S MISSION

Thinking with God's mind begins with an understanding of the Bible's overall missional message, from beginning to end. I recently traveled to India and met a professor and his wife who had moved there following retirement. Their reason? "Because this is where God is at work and we want to join Him." They had given up a comfortable retirement, left their children and grandchildren, and moved their huge library of several thousand volumes so they could equip young men and women to reach their nation with the gospel. Such commitment only comes in understanding the missional message of the Bible.

On Easter weekend, I asked some of my co-workers what they were doing for Easter. One person said she and her husband had invited some Chinese friends and their family to their home for "green tea and good news." They were serving tea and showing the *Jesus* video in Mandarin. Their Easter commitment was the result of understanding Scripture as the missions book of God.

The intentional plan of God is obvious as the Bible story again and again reveals mankind's failure before God and God's plan of redemption. Jesus made the intentional plan of God clear to those who listened to His teaching. He sought to open minds so His followers could understand Scripture in light of His life, death, and resurrection. He quoted from the Old Testament, bringing light to God's plan carried down through the ages and fulfilled in Him. H. Cornell Goerner writes in *All Nations in God's Purpose*, "It is a wonderful thing when the Lord can get our minds open, and then get us to open the Bible and place the open Bible in our opened minds."

Jesus traced God's plan through the books of Moses, the Prophets, and the Psalms. "Then he said to them, 'These are my words that I spoke to you while I was still with you—that everything written about me in the law of Moses, the prophets, and the psalms must be fulfilled'" (Luke 24:44). Jesus Himself followed the thread of God's plan from the beginning of Scripture to the end. He spent hours teaching His followers, opening their minds to see

God's plan and how that plan had been carried down from generation to generation. He made sure they understood God's mission.

Jesus identified two essential aspects of God's mission in Luke 24. First, Jesus explained that He would suffer, die, and rise again. "Then he opened their minds to understand the scriptures, and he said to them, Thus it is written, that the Messiah is to suffer and to rise from the dead on the third day" (Luke 24:45–46). Second, repentance and forgiveness were to be proclaimed in Jesus' name to all nations: "Repentance and forgiveness of sins is to be proclaimed in his name to all nations, beginning from Jerusalem" (Luke 24:47).

God's plan centered in Jesus and extended to the entire world. In the last hours of Jesus' life, He appeared to His disciples and stressed again the mission. "After he said this, he showed them his hands and his side. Then the disciples rejoiced when they saw the Lord. Jesus said to them again, 'Peace be with you. As the Father has sent me, so I send you'" (John 20:20–21).

Jesus explained and emphasized God's plan and our part again and again. He didn't leave any chance at all that we would not understand the intention of God's plan. Jesus prepared us to be as intentional in fulfilling God's plan as God was in revealing His plan through Jesus and His Word.

THE THREAD OF GOD'S LOVE IN SCRIPTURE

If someone asks you, "What is the Bible all about?" what would you say? W. O. Carver described the dominant theme of the Bible as "the major purpose of God and the universal outreach of his love." Carver held to a deep conviction that the Bible is a book about God's mission. According to Paul Borthwick in *A Mind for Missions*,

"The message of missions is woven throughout the Bible, and the sending of God's people into all the earth was not an appendix to the story of redemption. Missions was in God's heart all along. Our God is a missionary God!" In *Unveiled at Last*, Bob Sjogren writes that God's "Big Picture" is about "redeeming people from every tongue, tribe, and nation." The Bible is not to be read as 66 separate books, but as one book "to present a divine purpose of redeeming people from every tongue, tribe, and nation, resulting in a greater glory to the Lord through His creation as we now know it." Ralph Winter explains that the Bible belongs to all nations, for it is about the salvation plan for all peoples.

FROM THE BEGINNING

The love of God for the world and the sin that has stained every generation since creation are both spelled out in the first three chapters of Genesis. Yet God did not give up on mankind. He intervened again and again, providing a way for humanity to continue while at the same time hemming in the rampaging destruction of sin. He was setting the stage for His salvation plan that would be initiated in a man named Abram and fulfilled in a man named Jesus.

> *Now the Lord said to Abram, "Go from your country and your kindred and your father's house to the land that I will show you. I will make of you a great nation, and I will bless you, and make your name great, so that you will be a blessing. I will bless those who bless you, and the one who curses you I will curse; and in you all the families of the earth shall be blessed."*
>
> —Genesis 12:1–3

God made a covenant with Abraham, a covenant for all generations of people who love God. God blessed Abraham so he could be a blessing, and in the same way, God blesses us, intending that we also bless others. Scripture helps us see that intentional living includes being blessed and blessing others.

BLESSED TO BE A BLESSING

God sent Abram away from his country and his father's house "to the land that I will show you" (Genesis 12:1). He commissioned Abram with a two-part message. In *Unveiled at Last*, Bob Sjogren identifies the two parts as the top line and bottom line of God's plan. The top line is God's promised blessing to Abram. The bottom line is God's promise that Abram will be a blessing. In both parts of the commission, God is the initiator and the provider. God is a giving God who calls His followers to be giving people.

God is a giving God who calls His followers to be giving people.

Studies have shown that senior adults who have lived as "givers" will continue to invest themselves in others during their senior years. Because of this, they are the most fulfilled and satisfied with life. This same rule applies to believers; yet Christians often spend their lives in the "top line" of God's blessings, not realizing that the "bottom line" is where they will find their greatest blessing.

My friend Brunies has lived as a "giver" for over 80 years. Even today, I can't keep up with her! She overflows with God's blessings from her intentional commitment to live for His purposes. When she turned 80, she threw her own birthday party and invited a huge crowd to celebrate God's goodness in her life. She planned a day that would bless others and that would allow God's name to be glorified. That day was a shining testimony to intentional living. She has been investing her time, her heart, her energy, her money, and her life in sharing God's love for all her years. She doesn't wait for others to give her a reason to get up in the morning, or to invest herself in others. Her motivation is God's blessings, and she has developed a lifetime habit of giving to others what God has given to her. I know few people as satisfied with life as she is.

From the beginning God was giving, and when He created mankind in His image, He created us as giving creatures. God's story is the story of His lavish giving and our receiving, but it is also the story of our receiving and then letting the riches of God's blessing overflow on all those around us. God's blessings include grace, forgiveness, mercy, justice, strength, love, kindness, patience . . . and the list goes on. God gives us riches far greater than financial wealth or prestige.

The Bible story from the beginning is one of a loving Father blessing us. As our Abba blesses us, we are to bless others in the same way.

UNDERSTANDING THE BLESSING

Blessing is a term that is not as common to our contemporary use of language as it was in biblical times. A few years ago the concept of blessing was brought back to us when Gary Smalley and John Trent wrote the book *The Gift of the Blessing.* "To value something means to attach honor to it. In fact, this is the meaning of the verb 'to bless.' In Hebrew, the word *bless* literally means 'to bow the knee.' This word was used in showing reverence, even awe, to an important person. Now, this doesn't mean that in order to bless a person we are to stand back, fall to our knees, and bow before that person in awe!" Rather, blessing refers to God's original plan for mankind. It infers a life commitment to God's purposes, as well as a promise of God's active presence and direction as we fulfill His mission.

We pray for God's blessing on others, and ourselves, but we seldom consider what it might mean if God were to answer our prayers. What do we think will happen if God blesses others? How will that blessing look? What do we want to see happen in their lives? We seldom think about our own potential to be a blessing, or our need to be *intentional* about blessing others in our home, community, and workplace. When we pray or sing, "Lord, make me a blessing for someone today," what are we anticipating will occur, and what is our responsibility in that prayer?

Scripture helps us to understand what being a blessing looks like.

I am the Lord, I have called you in righteousness, I have taken you by the hand and kept you; I have given you as a covenant to the people, a light to the nations, to open the eyes that are blind, to bring out the prisoners from the dungeon, from the prison those who sit in darkness.

—Isaiah 42:6–7

Blessing takes the form of active involvement in bringing light to a dark world, a world darkened by social injustice and spiritual poverty, a world in need of God's presence.

God's presence and leading is promised to those who accept this commission and commit to fulfill the purpose for which God has created them, sent them, and blessed them. "I will lead the blind by a road they do not know, says the Lord" (Isaiah 42:16). "Do not fear, for I am with you" (Isaiah 43:5). "You are my witnesses" (Isaiah 43:10). God knows we cannot plan for the future. He understands that we do not know the way we should go.

Therefore, He assures us that He is the guide, He is the planner, He is already ahead of us charting out the course for our lives. The Lord makes it abundantly clear that we can have confidence in accepting His blessing and, in turn, becoming a blessing to others.

> *Blessing is not passive, but active involvement in other lives to bring them to the fullest measure of God's intention.*

Perhaps you are beginning to see that blessing is not passive, but active involvement in other lives to bring them to the fullest measure of God's intention. The peoples of the world that I am to bless may live in the house next door to me, or be in a refugee camp in the Sudan. The blessings I am to give bring healing and hope, mercy and justice, love and transformation, both of lives and societies. Above all else, all true blessings point people to God and His salvation offered in Jesus Christ. Intentional living is a life of receiving blessing from God and becoming a blessing to the world.

The Blessing Illuminated by Scripture

Thomas A. Jackson's hymn "We Are Called to Be God's People" provides a beautiful summary of God's blessing on His people. The three verses of the hymn identify our blessing from God in three ways: we are called to be God's people, God's servants, and God's prophets.

The Apostle Peter provides a very similar summary in 1 Peter 2:9: "But you are a chosen race, a royal priesthood, a holy nation, God's own people, in order that you may proclaim the mighty acts of him who called you out of darkness into his marvelous light."

The Apostle John describes God's people as "a kingdom and priests serving our God" (Revelation 5:10).

Perhaps you have not thought of being God's people, God's servants, and God's prophets as blessings, but *blessing* is what God is about as He calls us to these incredible roles at the heart of His mission. Bible study helps us to understand what it means to belong to God, to serve God, and to be a prophet of God—three important roles for all who choose to live for God's purposes. As Rick Warren writes in *The Purpose-Driven Life,* "To discover your purpose in life you must turn to God's Word, not the world's wisdom." Therefore, it only makes sense that the Bible is where we begin to understand that we have been blessed, and what this blessing includes.

BLESSED TO BE GOD'S PEOPLE

The greatest of all blessings is to belong to God, to be chosen by God. As the Lord led the Israelites out of bondage in Egypt to a place of freedom, He also clearly identified His intention that they would belong to Him from now on. From all the peoples of the earth, He set them aside as His own possession.

> *Now therefore, if you obey my voice and keep my covenant, you shall be my treasured possession out of all the peoples. Indeed, the whole earth is mine, but you shall be for me a priestly kingdom and a holy nation.*
>
> —Exodus 19:5–6

After the Israelites arrived in Canaan, after they failed to keep the covenant, after they failed to accept God's gracious blessing of belonging to Him, and while their lives spiraled further and further from God's intention for them, still He confirmed their divine ownership through the prophet Isaiah.

I have put my words in your mouth, and hidden you in the shadow of my hand, stretching out the heavens and laying the foundations of the earth, and saying to Zion, "You are my people."

—Isaiah 51:16

God doesn't give up on His people. He holds to His end of the covenant with a tenacious love that continues to find a way through sin and sorrow. He knew before the earth's foundations were in place that He would have to go the second and third mile with His chosen people, that He would have to make the greatest of all sacrifices to help His people fulfill their side of the covenant. In fact, God had already decided to send Jesus as a new covenant to replace the covenant that His people could not keep. God in His grace allowed Jesus to mend the broken covenant with His life, death, and resurrection. Jesus made it possible for all who believe to belong to God.

Jesus said to him, "'I am the way, and the truth, and the life. No one comes to the Father except through me. If you know me, you will know my Father also. From now on you do know him and have seen him.'"

—John 14:6–7

In a world of several billion people, spiritual loneliness is the greatest issue. Every physical need can be met, every social and educational opportunity can be provided, and the world can give both power and prestige . . . and still, every person not belonging to God is alone, completely alone.

Those of us who belong to God take for granted this belonging, this reality that we are never alone. We have a

Father who is with us wherever we are and whatever we face, a Father who actually has power over all situations, who does come to our rescue.

Our belonging to God is God's work. He chooses us. The Old Testament identified the Israelites as the people chosen by God to represent Him to the world. In the New Testament, Jesus Christ makes it possible for all people who trust in God to belong to Him. God chooses us because we believe in Christ.

> *Blessed be the God and Father of our Lord Jesus Christ, who has blessed us in Christ with every spiritual blessing in the heavenly places, just as he chose us in Christ before the foundation of the world to be holy and blameless before him in love. He destines us for adoption as his children through Jesus Christ, according to the good pleasure of his will, to the praise of his glorious grace that he freely bestowed on us in the Beloved.*
>
> —Ephesians 1:3–6

I have many friends with adopted children, but sometimes I forget who they are. Their children so completely *belong* that they appear to have been physically born into their new homes. Even those children who come from other cultures seem to have been grafted into their new families from before their birth.

The intentional decision we each make is whether we will accept God's offer to belong to Him in Christ. Will we choose to let God give us the blessing of becoming His people? We must accept this blessing for God to give us any of the other blessings that come from Him. Only as God's people do we discover the blessing of becoming God's servants.

Blessed to Be God's Servants

God's people are identified by whom they serve, and this is revealed in what they do and how they live. "How does God's love abide in anyone who has the world's goods and sees a brother or sister in need and yet refuses to help? . . . All who obey his commandments abide in him, and he abides in them" (1 John 3:17,24).

If you've paid attention to political elections, you've realized that the people who support a particular candidate can be identified because they are serving his or her cause. They speak for the candidate's platform and commit to the candidate's vision. But we seldom know whether their lives reflect the values and policies they propose.

God's people are different. Their life commitment is to serve God. God's concerns of love, justice, and righteousness identify God's servants. Scripture clearly identifies these as the issues that God's people are to be concerned with and to represent. Yes, they use words that come from God, but more than that, they live in such a way that God's "platform" can be seen in their actions. They are God's servants, and they like nothing better than pleasing Him. They live for God's desire.

God is looking for those who make an intentional decision to be His servants. He promises great blessings in return. "Your ancient ruins shall be rebuilt; you shall raise up the foundations of many generations; you shall be called the repairer of the breach, the restorer of streets to live in" (Isaiah 58:12). What a promise for those who make the intentional decision to invest their lives in love, justice, and righteousness! Can you imagine anything more wonderful than this promise of God to us?

Recently I stood in Corinth at the place where archaeologists uncovered an inscription of Erastus the city treasurer, who out of his own money had laid a portion of the road where the inscription was found. Erastus was a believer mentioned three times by the Apostle Paul. He was a committed witness to Christ who became a servant to the city where he served as trea-surer.

You and I may not have the money of Erastus to pay for the building of a city road, but according to God's promise as stated above, God has the resources to build a road that extends across generations, if we are willing to be the builders. He has the resources to free the oppressed, feed the hungry, cover the naked, heal the sick, vindicate the innocent, shield the threatened, and answer the calls for

> *God has the resources needed to transform the world, if only His servants are willing to bow before Him and say to Him, "Here am I."*

help. He has the resources needed to transform the world, if only His servants are willing to bow before Him and say to Him, "Here am I" (Isaiah 6:8).

BLESSED TO BE PROPHET AND PRIEST
Blessed to Be Prophet

Do you find it hard to imagine that God has blessed you to follow in the footsteps of men like Elijah, Isaiah, Amos, and Jeremiah? Just as Jeremiah was called to be a "prophet to the nations," we also are blessed with the same accountability. God's people are truly blessed to be the bearers of God's message. We are chosen as God's own people "in order that you may proclaim the mighty acts of him who called you out of darkness into his marvelous light" (1 Peter 2:9). Clearly, belonging to God is a public declaration! God's people are to tell the story that comes from God's heart. How long has it been since you proclaimed God's story? Intentional living assures that we will take every opportunity to express God's love through our words and actions.

I encounter prophets among God's people in many places. These are the ones who are not afraid to speak up about love, justice, and righteousness. They aren't afraid to take a stand, yet they are also involved in redemptive ministries. My friend Sister Chris ministered for years on death row in a Kentucky prison. Her ministry has not only included ministry to the prisoners, but also advocacy on their behalf.

Intentional living assures we will take every opportunity to express God's love through our words and actions.

The prophetic voice is often an unpopular voice. Isaiah denounced the oppression that denied justice and robbed the poor. Amos preached against the rejection of God's laws and the devaluing of human life. Jeremiah paid a price for describing the unfaithfulness of Israel and Judah as adulterous rejection of God, for "their wickedness in forsaking me; they have made offerings to other gods, and worshiped the works of their own hands" (Jeremiah 1:16). People do not want to be deterred from their own desires.

The Old Testament prophets brought the message of judgment, but they also brought a message of hope. Isaiah painted a picture of expansion and renewal: "Enlarge the site of your tent, and let the curtains of your habitations be stretched out; do not hold back; lengthen your cords and strengthen your stakes. For you will spread out to the right and to the left, and your descendants will possess the nations and will settle the desolate towns" (Isaiah 54:2).

Jeremiah gave assurance of a future restoration: "For surely I know the plans I have for you, says the Lord, plans for your welfare and not for harm, to give you a future with hope. Then when you call upon me and come and pray to me, I will hear you. When you search for me, you will find me; if you seek me with all your heart, I will let you find me, says the LORD, and I will restore your fortunes and gather you from all the nations and all the places where I have driven you, says the LORD, and I will bring you back to the place from which I sent you into exile" (Jeremiah 29:11–14).

Amos proclaims the good news of coming prosperity and permanence: "I will restore the fortunes of my people Israel, and they shall rebuild the ruined cities and inhabit them; they shall plant vineyards and drink their wine, and they shall make gardens and eat their fruit. I will plant them upon their land, and they shall never again be plucked up out of the land that I have given them, says the LORD your God" (Amos 9:14–15).

Representing God as His prophet is not only a blessing, but an honor. If God has given you His message to deliver, you will experience fulfillment in life as you follow His plan. Unless God's prophets are willing to deliver God's message, those who have turned away from God will be denied the joy of returning to their Lord and Maker. They will never know the joy of the Lord. Since the gospel is good news, we can rest assured that God's judgment is always accompanied with grace and hope for an abundant life.

Blessed to Be Priest

"Pray for me!" was the plea of an email that I received from an individual who had heard me speak. She sought me out, knowing that I could intercede with her and for her. Not because I am ordained, or because I am on a church staff, or because I have a seminary degree, but because I am a fellow believer, one of God's own people, one of "a royal priesthood" with direct access to God in Jesus Christ.

We have access to God and we have a responsibility to bring others to Him. Whereas the Old Testament covenant provided for only those who had the formal title of high priest to enter into the Holy of Holies, now we, because of Jesus Christ, can come before the throne of God. Now Jesus Himself is our mediator.

Do you realize the blessing that this is? You and I, clay vessels, flesh and blood, can approach the Lord of lords, the Creator of the universe! But our blessing doesn't stop there. We also have the honor of bringing others before God, introducing them to our Lord, interceding for them and blessing them in the same way that God has blessed us.

You may recall that the priest of the old covenant brought animal and plant sacrifices to God. Blood had to be shed for forgiveness to be given. But because of Christ, we now have only to bring ourselves: "I appeal to you therefore, brothers and sisters, by the mercies of God, to present your bodies as a living sacrifice, holy and acceptable to God, which is your spiritual worship" (Romans 12:1). Our offering is ourselves—all that we are, all that we have, and all that we hope to be. Our offerings come from a heart full of gratitude for the goodness of God to us. Our gratitude moves us to serve God and proclaim the good news of His salvation to the entire world.

We are surely blessed to be counted among God's people, to be honored as His servant, and to proclaim the good news of His love so that others might have what we have been given. Somewhere in your daily experience, there are people waiting to be blessed by God through you. Don't you want to be a person who blesses others? If so, decide today to explore God's Word more fully to discover what people who bless others look like. Make it your intention to learn to think with God's mind.

THE MIND OF CHRIST

The Bible is God's missions book. He has laid out His plan so we can understand and be involved. Yet fully understanding His mission takes concerted study and guidance of the Holy Spirit. The Spirit is our teacher, allowing us to see the deep truths of God and giving us the strength and wisdom to put these truths to work in our lives. The Apostle Paul understood that we could only think with God's mind as we surrender to the leadership of the Spirit in all we do. "Those who are spiritual discern all things, and they are themselves subject to no one else's scrutiny. 'For who has known the mind of the Lord so as to instruct him?' But we have the mind of Christ" (1 Corinthians 2:15–16). Thinking with God's mind is an intentional commitment to learn more of Him and His Word.

Thinking with God's Mind
"'I have called you friends, because I have made known to you everything that I have heard from my Father'" (John 15:15). Look for God's mission in every verse of Scripture. Learn what God has to say to you about living intentionally for His purposes.

SEEING THROUGH GOD'S EYES:

Worldview

*R*un to and fro through the streets of Jerusalem,
    look around and take note!
Search its squares and see if you can find one person
    who acts justly and seeks truth—
so that I may pardon Jerusalem. . . .
O Lord, do your eyes not look for truth?
You have struck them,
    but they felt no anguish;
you have consumed them,
    but they refused to take correction.
They have made their faces harder than rock;
    they have refused to turn back.
Then I said, "These are only the poor,
    they have no sense;
for they do not know the way of the Lord,
    the law of their God.
Let me go to the rich and speak to them;
surely they know the way of the Lord,
    the law of their God."
But they all alike had broken the yoke,
    they had burst the bonds.

—Jeremiah 5:1,3—5

Seeing Through God's Eyes

There is a yearning in the very core of the heart to rest in some understanding of the alpha and omega of the human condition.

—David Naugle, *Worldview: The History of a Concept*

Could you explain your worldview if asked? A single word might reveal something of your view. For instance, is there such as thing as a *secular* job for a Christian? Are there any *absolutes* in life? Is our faith a *private* matter? Is Jesus the *only* way to God? Is Christianity about *service* or *authority*? What does *family* mean? How does a Christian live out being a *citizen*? How should I feel about *foreigners*? You could continue this list with dozens of questions that reveal something about your view of life. Do your answers to these questions reflect an intentional commitment to see life through God's eyes? Or do you suspect that some areas of your worldview need the transforming work of God?

Scripture explains that God's view is transformational, for He moves us away from our self-centeredness to a loving and compassionate response to the hurting and the lost. John 3:16 speaks of a love for the world that is so deep, so profound, so passionate and compassionate that God willingly gives His "one of a kind Son." Only as our worldview is enlarged, changed, or even revolutionized do we begin to understand that God is revealing His love to the world, and He wants us to join Him in what He is doing.

Everyone has a worldview, or a way that they interpret reality and view life. A brief conversation often begins to reveal a person's worldview, even though that person may not realize they have one. Depending on our worldview, we may approach others with love or disdain. We may show mercy or condemnation. We may view a crime as a social issue, a political issue, an economic issue, or a moral issue. We may take responsibility for the world we live in or blame the system. We may see our work as just a job or a place to make a difference. We may be givers or getters. We may live only for self or for a higher purpose.

> God moves us away from our self-centeredness to a loving and compassionate response to the hurting and the lost.

Trisa was painting in the sanctuary of our church on the day we met. Our friendship has lasted over 30 years; and during those years our life journeys have sent us in different directions, traveling to places around the world, both as teachers and learners. But regardless of how many places we may go, it is only as Christ transforms our view of life to be more like His that we experience wholeness and we can begin to make sense out of this world that we live in.

Since Trisa and I have been friends for all these years, I asked her to share one way God has continued to mold her view of life to be more like His. Trisa's story is a perfect illustration of what can happen when we open our minds and let God show us His world through His eyes.

~

TRISA'S STORY

My husband is the dean of the business school in a faith-based liberal arts college in Washington State. Before he took this position he was a professor in a similarly sized faith-based college in Texas. In the course of our ministry with young adults in Christian higher education, we have uncovered some troubling perceptions among business majors. One is that they have a sense of being second-class citizens in academia. They may, for instance, use disparaging qualifiers in describing their major: "I'm *just* a business major"; or, "Well, I couldn't seem to figure out what I wanted to do with my life—so I majored in business."

I was perplexed as to the source of this thinking. And then I began to listen very carefully to the dialogues in and about business: "The love of money is a root of all kinds of evil." "You cannot serve both God and wealth." "It is easier for a camel to go through the eye of a needle than for someone who is rich to enter the kingdom of God." Certainly these statements are canon. What dismays and disheartens is how often they are decontextualized. None of these statements from Scripture, when contextualized, disparage the accumulation of wealth. But each of them addresses in the strongest possible language the wrongly motivated aggregation of resources.

At some point we begin to equate poverty with virtue, but what in the world is virtuous about poverty? What is virtuous about a child dying every 15 seconds on this globe from the effects of drinking unsafe water? What is virtuous about more than 1 billion people, 16 percent of the human population, not having access to the basic social services of health care, education, safe drinking water, and adequate nutrition? What is virtuous about 1.1 billion people living on $1 per day? Poverty is *not* virtue, either in the developing world or the developed nations.

We have conceptual compassion for the poor, but zero compassion for the rich and powerful— even within our own ranks. In reality, those among us who spend Monday through Friday in the trenches of the secular world have infinitely more opportunities to share the gospel with the lost than do our pulpit ministers. We should be anointing and commissioning our marketplace ministers with all the fervor and ceremony with which we commission our pulpit ministers. We should be breathing daily blessing upon them as they venture into uncharted territory and do what no vocational pastor will ever have the opportunity to do.

Jesus said He came to preach good news to the poor. That good news is the alleviation of poverty in all of its forms, through His agents—you and me. That's going to require a course correction, a critical look at some old and antiquated theology. That's going to require a new worldview, seeing through God's eyes, capturing *His* worldview.

For years and years after I came into a saving relationship with Christ, I was perfectly able to simultaneously seek and disdain profit. My worldview didn't feel incongruent. I was confident that God would be far more pleased with a life of austerity and abstinence than any alternative. I sang the song of asceticism in full voice—and then figured out what I needed to do to feed, clothe, and shelter myself and have surplus for the needy. There didn't *seem* to be a disconnect. I was confident that, given enough time, I could weave these two threads as one; that what may have seemed a clash of theology or ideology to some could be harmoniously woven into a seamless amalgamation of Mother Teresa and Donald Trump. Oh my.

Our world is chaotic, broken, and seemingly ruined beyond redemption at times. But you know what? Nothing has changed in the heavenly places. God is on His throne. His plan continues to unfold. He is preparing a generation of amazing young adults with a brand-new worldview to thunder into that chaos with purpose and plan. In my little world, at this time and in this place, it means sharing these truths with young men and young women of faith, with a gift for business, who are full of promise and potential but who've been led to believe that anything they can do is less significant than those who are called to traditional Christian ministry. I can't wait to give them the good news! Once I allowed God to change *my* worldview, I was able to articulate it to others. I have seen the spark of hope and excitement in the eyes of young adults majoring in business as they come to a new understanding of business, wealth, capitalism, and our responsibility to a poor and hurting world. They can do it. I can do it. You can do it. Hallelujah!

∽

COMMITTED TO SEE AS GOD SEES

Certainly God shapes our worldview as we open our minds to let Him sort through the traditions and habits, the culture and context, to see what He is really about; or as Henry Blackaby says, to move us toward God's agenda. Our Lord eagerly awaits the day when we will become intentionally committed to see as He sees, to challenge our worldview assumptions so that He can open our eyes to His view.

In *Shaping a Christian Worldview*, David Dockery writes that how we understand the world has cosmic implications, for "there is a great spiritual battle raging for the hearts and minds of men and women around the globe." Dockery's words remind us of the ultimate result if God's people remain locked in "assumptions" that restrict their ability to respond to the great spiritual and physical needs in the world.

Most of us think that our view of life, how we see things, is the right view. Have you ever begun to tell someone a story from your past, only to have a family member correct the details, or your view of the event? Our view can be less than accurate, even of those things that we think we know best. If we aren't seeing our own lives accurately, it isn't hard to imagine that we are not seeing other people, other places, and other events—our world—flawlessly as well.

Often, based on what we have heard others say, we make assumptions that keep us from exploring our worldview to see where it might need a fuller understanding. We walk through life with assumptions about our lives and our world that "mold our thinking, shape our conclusions, and direct the decisions that lie behind our actions and attitudes," Christian Overman says in *Assumptions That Affect Our Lives*. For instance, without even realizing it, many Christians segment their lives into church, work, and home—a view that is inconsistent with Christian doctrine. We are God's ambassadors wherever we go. We are called to be on mission in our homes, our workplaces, and through our churches. Without a missional worldview, an understanding that the fragrance of Christ is to permeate all that we do in the way we work, live, and worship, we may never connect our daily lives with "God so loved the world."

Intentionally Testing Our Worldview

God's view of the world is the right view, and the more intimately we are involved with Him, the more clearly we will see His view. We must continually examine our worldview against Scripture, allowing the Holy Spirit to illumine our understanding and break through our assumptions.

We can challenge our attitudes, beliefs, assumptions, and values with four simple lines of questioning:

1. Where did it come from? Was it inherited? Did someone teach me this? Is it based on someone else's opinion or is it verified truth?

2. What is the consequence? If I continue in this manner, what will be the result for myself and for others?

3. Is it consistent with my overall worldview? Would I feel good about sharing this with other Christ followers, or do I feel embarrassed about it?

4. How do I feel when I act on it? Does it draw me closer to God or move me further from Him? Does it add value to life and affirm the value of others?

God's Absolutes

The world and the future of the world belong to God. Perhaps now more than ever, we need to know that God is still sovereign; has come in His Son, Jesus Christ; and has a plan for each individual, as well as mankind and the world in general. He has determined the absolutes, for He alone understands the way life should be lived and what He has intentioned for mankind.

The Absolute Sovereignty of God

God's Word clearly places God first in our lives. He is identified as the singular object of our affection. When Jesus was questioned concerning the greatest commandment, He answered, "The first is, 'Hear, O Israel: the Lord our God, the Lord is one; you shall love the Lord your God with all your heart, and with all your soul, and with all your mind, and with all your strength'" (Mark 12:29–30).

The Bible describes God as personal, unique, eternal, infinite, unchanging, holy, righteous, just, good, true, faithful, gracious, merciful, and all things good. He gives meaning and coherence to all things. God is the sovereign Creator and Sustainer of all life. He is Spirit, eternally existing in three unique personalities. "'Go therefore and make disciples of all nations, baptizing them in the name of the Father and of the Son and of the Holy Spirit'" (Matthew 28:19).

The Absolute Oneness and Fellowship of God

The oneness of God is evident in the eternal and divine nature of Jesus Christ and the Holy Spirit, eternally with God, eternally of God, eternally God. "In the beginning was the Word, and the Word was with God, and the Word was God. He was in the beginning with God" (John 1:1). God reveals His nature through this eternal relationship of Father, Son, and Spirit. "No one has ever seen God. It is God the only Son, who is close to the Father's heart, who has made him known" (John 1:18). God literally walked on earth in Jesus. "And the Word became flesh

God alone understands the way life should be lived and what He has intentioned for mankind.

and lived among us, and we have seen his glory, the glory of a father's only son, full of grace and truth" (John 1:14).

God is present and active in all places at all times in the person of the Holy Spirit, pointing people to God and indwelling those who trust in His love as revealed through the life, death, and resurrection of Jesus. "'When the Spirit of truth comes, he will guide you into all truth; for he will not speak on his own, but will speak whatever he hears, and he will declare to you the things that are to come. He will glorify me, because he will take what is mine and declare it to you'" (John 16:13–14).

The one true God revealed in the Three Persons of Father, Son, and Holy Spirit is an absolute. Seeing the

world through God's eyes is to see God as **"I AM WHO
I AM."** God's sovereignty, revealed through both flesh
and spirit, is the very thing that helps us make sense out of
life, for He alone has authority and power to offer us a
future and a hope (Jeremiah 29:11). He alone has the
plan for all of earth, for all of eternity.

The Absolute Way to God

Jesus is God's plan. He has been God's plan since the
beginning of time. God wants us to know Him and know
what pleases Him. God came to earth in human form so
we could understand His love, righteousness, and justice.

I had just spoken on proclamation to a gathering of
Catholic nuns and priests. As I walked to my seat, a precious elderly sister stopped me. She held my face in her
hands, her face glowing with the love of God, and said,
"It's all about Jesus." No truer words can be spoken when
it comes to seeing through God's eyes.

When my daughter was young, we lived in a community with a large number of people who attended the
Church of Jesus Christ of Latter-day Saints (LDS) church.
Early in life, she had schoolteachers and friends who
claimed that Jesus isn't the only Son of God and that He
is not the only way to God. She had to decide what she
would believe. Our family had opportunities to review
Scriptures that clearly identify Jesus as the Savior and
Lord, the only way to God, and the only One sent from
God through whom we find forgiveness and reconciliation
with God. According to Scripture, Jesus Christ is an
absolute. "God abides in those who confess that Jesus is
the Son of God, and they abide in God" (1 John 4:15).

What we do with Jesus is formative to our worldview.
The urgency of telling the world about Him is founded
on this single understanding. Seeing through God's eyes
reveals a world in desperate need of Jesus, their only hope
for life and eternity. "'For God so loved the world that he

gave his only Son, so that everyone who believes in him may not perish but may have eternal life'" (John 3:16).

The Absolute Grace and Provision of God

God's concern is seen at two levels. His first concern is the gulf of sin that has separated humanity from God. According to Scripture, every person has sinned and is separated from God. Sin is any choice made in life that is not according to God's will. Sin is living for one's self rather than God's plan. Sin is our failure to give our lives totally over to God's loving care.

The perfection of God requires the highest penalty for sin—eternal death and separation from God. "There is no distinction, since all have sinned and fall short of the glory of God. . . . For the wages of sin is death, but the free gift of God is eternal life in Christ Jesus our Lord" (Romans 3:22–23; 6:23).

Were it not for God's grace, humankind would be in a desperate situation, for we are not able to free ourselves from sinful behavior. Only a divine Savior could accomplish such a feat. Jesus, God's Son, was that Savior. Jesus came as the bridge over which we can come again to God. The Apostle John described Jesus as "the righteous; and he is the atoning sacrifice for our sins, and not for ours only but also for the sins of the whole world" (1 John 2:1–2).

Jesus lived victoriously. He died victoriously. And He conquered death victoriously. Jesus is the Savior of the world! God views the world through the shed blood of Jesus; and because of this, those who claim Jesus as Lord are seen in light of the righteousness of Christ.

God's second concern is the result of our sinfulness— the brokenness of humanity in caring for one another and the world God has blessed us with. Seeing the world through God's eyes reveals God's concern for issues that affect our world every day. When our worldview is in line with God's view, our concerns are the same as His. Seeing the world through God's eyes will affect how we view hunger, poverty, justice, education, finance, sex, family, abuse, freedom, separation of church and state, politics, governments, democracy, capitalism, war, prejudice, hatred . . . and the list goes on. These involve life situations that affect us every day and have moral elements. We may find ourselves on opposite sides of the ethical debates with our best friends; and even when we hold the same values, we may disagree on how to bring transformation. The immense complexity of life issues requires wisdom and courage available only from God as He enables us to see through the lens of His steadfast love, justice, and righteousness.

> *When our worldview is in line with God's view, our concerns are the same as His.*

Some of the questions we must begin to ask and to contemplate with one another will perhaps free us as believers to pursue God's view more clearly.

• How does the legislation in our country affect the poorest of the poor, children, displaced people, and those who cannot speak for themselves?

• How are our churches structured to enable their congregations to become involved in the transformation of cities, business, and government?

• How does a nation reflect Christian values and still provide freedom of belief and practice?

• How do Christians become powerful influencers of society? What does the church look like when it is the influencer rather than the influenced?

• What should the global mission of God look like in the twenty-first century?

When we understand that God is concerned with the issues of life, we then begin to grasp that He is indeed involved with our entire lives—including our homes and our work. Our response must be an intentional decision to see all of life through the divine lens of God.

GOD'S VIEW OF HOME

Susan Field, in *My Children, My Mission Field*, identifies our homes and families as the beginning and primary place for fulfilling God's mission. She reminds us that God has already charted plans for our lives that "are ultimately valuable to the kingdom of God." Seeing the world through God's eyes has tremendous implications for family. I remember hearing of one family whose giving at Christmas instilled in their preschooler a desire to give all he had for missionary support.

The Christian missions organization WMU® offers families opportunities to do volunteer missions together for a weekend. Each volunteer experience is designed to allow families to participate in a variety of ministry and evangelism projects already planned by the churches in the area. Called FamilyFest, these volunteer missions events are encouraging families to do missions together, so that they grow in their ability to see the world through God's eyes.

Have you noticed a difference in children raised in homes where giving, ministering, and sharing Christ are part of their home life? Field writes, "As you look on the precious faces of your children, visualize them walking the path God has laid out for them. Remind yourself of how much your own love for them mirrors the love of God for them and the love of God for you." The investment that parents make in the creation of a home with missional values is an investment that comes from hearts filled with love for God and His purposes. Children with such values do not happen by accident. Rather, such children come from homes that make intentional decisions to give, minister, and share Christ—in other words, intentional decisions to live for the purposes of God.

GOD'S VIEW OF WORK

Trisa's story earlier in this chapter is a reminder that our assumptions can keep us from seeing what God really wants to do through us. So often I have had people tell me how much they would like to work where I work so they could be involved in ministry. These comments have allowed me to affirm their work as their mission, right where they are—in homes and offices where people need Christ, where people need to see truth and compassion lived out in the lives of those around them. The assumption that one must work in a Christian organization to be in ministry is one worldview that keeps God's people from engaging His mission where they live and work. Christians begin to think that missionaries and ministers are professionals with a calling and accountability that others do not have.

Dennis Bakke, president and CEO of Imagine Schools, affirms in his book *Joy at Work* that our workplace is our mission, the very place where we are to use our God-given talents to shape society and serve mankind. His testimony affirms his lifelong intention of breaking down the wall between the secular and the spiritual. "Growing up in a Christian home, Bakke noticed that people seemed to get more credit for contributing to society if they did it within a Christian rather than a secular context. . . . Bakke always wanted to do something useful for society and felt called to service in the secular arena, but he never believed that work in government or business would be as honorable as church work. Searching for intersections between his desire to contribute, his calling, and his faith, he joined Christian Bible study and discussion groups and began to formulate a values- and principles-based approach to business. 'God is not a typical boss,' Bakke writes. 'God delegated decision making to humans from their introduction in Eden. Adam's and Eve's jobs, and those of all humans who followed them, were to act as stewards—that is, keepers of the Earth and all that was created there. God appears pleased by all human work, not preferring one type over another. All kinds of production and management activities appear to honor and please the Creator, particularly if they please the person who does them.'"

Allowing God to break down the wall we build between our work and our spirituality is more difficult than most of us think. Some who work in schools or government tell me they are unable to be a witness for Christ, while others find innumerable ways to show and live out their faith. The latter group is intentional in viewing their workplace as their place to fulfill God's mission, which opens their eyes to creative methods and God-given opportunities.

As I walked to the first session of a large Christian conference, I began to chat with a young man in the hallway. Since most of the attendees were pastors, I asked if he was a pastor, and he answered apologetically, "No, I am just in sales. I'm not in the ministry." As Trisa has discovered in her experience, this young man did not see his work as having value in comparison to the work of the pastors attending the event. I stopped and commissioned him to his workplace, praying that he would be God's ambassador and that many would be turned to God because of his faith and witness.

The young man was surprised. I saw him several times between sessions, and each time he expressed what that had meant to him. I can't wait to see what God will do through him now that he knows God has an intentional plan for him right where he is, now that he knows he can live intentionally for God's mission through his work. His *workview* (my newly coined word!), his worldview, has been transformed!

IS OUR VIEW GOD'S VIEW?

My daughter decided to keep her children in public school after thoughtfully considering homeschooling. She was concerned about school policies that nearly prohibit any activity that reflects Christian beliefs. But rather than pull her children from the school, she committed to active involvement in school activities. When her youngest child entered kindergarten, she decided to become a teacher's aide for special-needs children at the middle school her two older children attend.

Although Michele had often volunteered to help at the school before, for the first time she became a spectator to the daily inner world that her children and the teachers faced. She discovered a place in need of Christian influence and presence. She found teachers seeking to make a difference in a system often plagued by obstacles to success. God has placed her where she might be a catalyst for spiritual change, a ray of light in the midst of darkness.

Whatever our situation, God must change our view if we are to see with His eyes. We cannot turn away from the needs of the world or hide comfortably in our living rooms if we are to be intentional about seeing through God's eyes. Our televisions offer many opportunities to see the broken world, but usually it will take more than a television program to transform our worldview.

THE TRANSFORMATIONAL RESULT OF SEEING THROUGH GOD'S EYES

Our view of global concerns has a direct implication for how we live and how we fulfill God's missions plan. From the time we are young, our parents or caregivers are influencing our attitudes, beliefs, and values. As we mature, teachers, friends, media, and our own experiences influence us. Yet all of these influences are secondary to understanding God's view. When we understand that God is concerned for all people, and that His intent is love, justice, and righteousness for all, we begin to realize that love, justice, and righteousness take shape as we engage the concerns that face people in their daily lives. Jesus didn't take us out of the world. Rather, He left us in the world so we could go into the world, into our Jerusalem, our Judea, our Samaria, and our uttermost parts of the earth.

We cannot hide comfortably in our living rooms if we are to be intentional about seeing through God's eyes.

Our actions are the clearest picture of how we see the world. History tells the story of women and men who stood to the death for God's purposes in this world. They went wherever God sent them, delivered the message God gave them, met the needs God showed them, and left God's imprint wherever they were. They made an intentional decision to see the world through God's eyes.

CAN GOD CHANGE MY VIEW?

I was in an airplane somewhere over Wyoming when God spoke to me. I had been staying in the home of a couple who began each day in prayer for the peoples of the world and the Christians reaching out to them. My worldview had been changed, for I discovered that praying for the world was an intentional daily commitment that would change my worldview, that would open my heart to see the world through God's eyes.

When I arrived home, I knew that praying for the peoples of the world had to become an intentional part of my life. And even beyond that, I realized that as a believer I needed to know what God was about in other places beyond my immediate community, my state, or even my nation. The Lord wanted me to join Him in letting the world know of His love in Jesus Christ.

Sometimes God catches our attention and reveals our need for an expanded view. He puts us in situations where we are confronted by our myopic view of life. At the same time, we can make some intentional decisions that will encourage us to see the world through God's eyes.

1. Observe the world around you. Look to see where God is at work. What is happening and what is He saying to you? How would you have to change to join Him in His work?

2. Discuss the important issues related to love, justice, and righteousness with people who agree and disagree. What have they discovered in Scripture? What have they learned from other sources? What is causing you to agree or disagree with their views?

3. Evaluate Christian response to the spiritual and physical needs of our world. What is working and what isn't working? What resources do you have that need to be given to God?

4. Listen for God's encouragement, guidance, and command. What would it look like for you to be obedient?

5. Accept someone who is different from you. Take an intentional action that affirms their value. What barriers are you willing cross to do this?

6. Spend time alone with God, letting Him love you and teach you, that you might see through His eyes. Does His view move you to compassionate action?

The volunteer missions team I led to Athens, Greece, attended the Greek Evangelical Church on our first Sunday there. A young man from Scotland preached in

English while the Greek pastor interpreted into Greek for the church members. The congregation was a blend of Greek, Brazilian, American, and Scottish believers. The Scripture passage was familiar, but hearing it in a different context allowed at least one of the team members to see the world through God's eyes in a new way. Here is what Christina wrote about that morning.

~

CHRISTINA'S STORY

I am a PK and grew up in a home full of love and God my entire life. My parents were missionaries to Brazil for three years, and I have heard every way to tell someone about the gospel. I can give you every "Sunday School" answer to any question you have, but this trip to Greece changed my life. I knew it was going to when on the first day I heard a sermon on Scriptures that I had heard more times than I can count, but I finally got it.

Ian spoke on several Scriptures from Luke about how God was taken to different people. Luke 4:14–21 is where Jesus read from the scroll in the Book of Isaiah. Verses 18–19 say, "God's spirit is on me; he's chosen me to preach the Message of good news to the poor, . . . to announce, 'This is God's year to act!'" (*The Message*). I really feel, just as Jesus said in verse 21, that this Scripture came true before my very eyes. I was sent to Greece to share and to encourage others to hear because this *is* the year to act.

It was all summed up in something Ian said. He commented on the fact that there were at least three countries represented in the service that morning. He said, "We are all from different countries, but all who follow Christ are from Him. We are all His ambassadors. We are all His representatives. When others see us, they should see Him."

Choosing to see the world through God's eyes is an intentional decision. Christina has made her decision. How about you?

Seeing Through God's Eyes
Be on the watch for assumptions about God, people, and the world that may keep you from fully claiming your part of God's plan. We can easily become scoffers when we are confronted by realities that are different from what we have been taught. Paul faced this in Athens in response to the message he preached at Mars Hill. "When they heard of the resurrection of the dead, some scoffed; but others said, 'We will hear you again about this'" (Acts 17:32).

Our God invites us into a unique culture described as the kingdom of God. Are you scoffing at something that is in truth God seeking to break you out of your assumptions to discover a new reality and truth of Him?

LOVING WITH GOD'S HEART:
Relationships

or though I am free with respect to all, I have made myself a slave to all, so that I might win more of them. To the Jews I became as a Jew, in order to win Jews. To those under the law, I became as one under the law (though I myself am not under the law) so that I might win those under the law. To those outside the law, I became as one outside the law (though I am not free from God's law but am under Christ's law) so that I might win those outside the law. To the weak I became weak, so that I might win the weak. I have become all things to all people, that I might by all means save some. I do it all for the sake of the gospel, so that I may share in its blessings.

—1 Corinthians 9:19—23

LOVING WITH GOD'S HEART

Who would be better than the Christian community to lead society in the development of successful, healthy cross-cultural relationships?

—Patty Lane, *A Beginner's Guide to Crossing Cultures*

Your love of God is shown to Him through your love of others. He asks that you let His love be evident through you. It is not your love but His love that enables you to be a good neighbor. God's love for us calls us to an intentional choice to love others.

Jesus declared that love of God and love of others were the first and second greatest commandments. Jesus told the story of the Samaritan who turned aside to help a wounded man by the side of the road. The story clearly condemns the actions of the priest and the Levite, both of whom "passed by on the other side" (Luke 10:31–32). The actions of the Samaritan affirm the intentions of God that we cross barriers that separate us from others, whatever those barriers might be. This story alone suggests barriers of class, race, religion, and culture, just to name a few. When we love God, we are also lovers of people.

When Jesus led His disciples into Samaria, they were slow to comprehend that the barriers of race, religion, and culture could not and should not stand in the way of God's love for all people. Jesus showed them how to cross barriers that separated people from God and from one another. Then He sent them out by twos to do the same.

In this same way, God's people are to look for ways to cross barriers so persons of other cultures or lifestyles may know Christ. They discern, empathize, and take action regarding the spiritual and physical needs of the peoples to whom they are called.

In Luke 4:18, Jesus sets forth His intention, an intention He commands us to adopt as our own.

"The Spirit of the Lord is upon me, because he has anointed me to bring good news to the poor. He has sent me to proclaim release to the captives and recovery of sight to the blind, to let the oppressed go free, to proclaim the year of the Lord's favor."

When Christians act to bring barriers down, God empowers His people to truly transform lives and nations. Yet, for over 2,000 years God's people have been slow to believe what Jesus taught. Tearing down walls and becoming partners is the biblical model. The early church discovered early on that they were not only to embrace the Jews, but also the Gentiles. When Peter went to the house of the Gentile Cornelius, he saw the Holy Spirit come upon Cornelius, his family, and his close friends. Then Paul reported that he was called to the Gentiles. The first Christians had to come to terms with this unexpected outpouring of God's love and Spirit on people they considered unclean. But they could not deny what they saw happen.

Paul explained that in Christ we become one. All barriers are removed. A new culture has come in Christ, a spiritual culture that overcomes all physical barriers.

But now in Christ Jesus you who once were far off have been brought near by the blood of Christ. For his is our peace; in his flesh he has made both groups into one and has broken down the dividing wall, that is, the hostility between us.

—Ephesians 2:13–14

Barriers come in many forms. What I consider a difficult barrier may not be hard for you at all. But for God's purposes to be fulfilled, we all must cross barriers that keep us from going to those who need to be blessed.

Consider in your own life the barriers that you face. How intentional are you in letting God lead you to reach across barriers to share His love through your life and words?

SOCIAL BARRIERS

When I was invited to join a ministry to topless dancers in my community, I hesitated. Going into a nightclub would require crossing a social and moral barrier that I wasn't sure I could or should cross. Yet, with some fear and uncertainty, and an assurance from God that He was leading, I said yes.

The director of the ministry prepared me for the nightclub culture. Our goal, she explained, was to personally affirm the women, build relationships, and provide a witness for Christ as we had opportunity. Our job wasn't to judge or condemn, but to love and minister. Common problems among dancers included low esteem, alcoholism, and drug addiction. Their chosen path could not fulfill their dreams.

Each of us involved in the ministry enlisted at least three people who would pray specifically for us on the days we entered the clubs. From my first visit, I realized why the pray-ers were critical—this was spiritual warfare. The nightclub's lack of physical light only emphasized the intense spiritual darkness that hung heavily in the air. No doubt, the prayers of my friends allowed me to experience God's peace, even as I sat looking at the sad state of human life around me.

The situation was sad. Beautiful women with so much

to offer, settling for far less than the life God had planned for them, moved me to tears. But as they came to our table to visit with us, I was filled with love for these women, women with stories, women with hopes and needs, women like every woman I had ever met.

God's love for these women led me to an intentional decision to continue to cross this social and moral barrier to touch the lives of the women who lived on the other side. God wants them to know His love, a love that is deep enough, wide enough, long enough, and high enough to cross any barrier, a love that will reach to them right where they are and lift them to God.

Jesus crossed barriers to reach tax collectors, adulterous women, and prostitutes. He said, "'Let anyone among you who is without sin be the first to throw a stone.'" In other words, judgment of others isn't what we are to be about. We are to bring love and forgiveness.

Loving with God's heart is all about God's love. When we make the intentional decision to live for God's purposes, we begin to understand our need to also love with God's heart, for we cannot love as we should on our own. Our intention must be to love with God's love, for His love is the only love powerful enough to transform our lives and the lives of those around us.

DISTANCE AND LANGUAGE BARRIERS

I've known Ken and Cathy since before they were married over 20 years ago, and I have watched them grow as they moved toward God's purposes for their lives. In college Ken committed to God to pursue missions. On a missions trip several years later, Ken met Cathy, who was also committed to missions. As the couple prepared over the next several years and looked forward to their future as missionaries, they faced many obstacles, including the loss of dear family members and setbacks with their mission-sending agency. Beyond even these issues, however, Ken and Cathy needed to be willing to leave their families and learn a new language if they were going to reach people for God in faraway places. The decision to cross distance and language barriers isn't easy, even when you know that it is God's plan for you. Yet, Ken and Cathy made the intentional decision to cross the barriers before them, for they chose to live for God's purposes rather than their own. They chose to love people in a distant place, who spoke another language, with God's heart.

~

Ken's Story

Sometimes the hardest thing in life is to see your dream come true. The opportunity was laid before us, but could I leave my parents? Could we take a growing family halfway around the world to Chile, to a new language, a new culture, and new challenges? God knew my thoughts. He was still leading. My parents were 100 percent supportive. Cathy's family was also behind our decision. And though it wasn't as easy as it would have been years earlier, God was still leading in the everlasting way.

We discovered that cross-cultural ministry is about making a conscious effort to make adjustments. The missionary who tries to work his pre-made plan does not last on the field. Those who come to learn and to see where God is at work will build the relationships necessary to see results. Relationships do not happen automatically, especially in Chile. You must make the first move if you expect to develop a relationship with anyone. Cathy and I are very intentional about adjusting our way of outreach to the needs of each community in which we minister. Through community development and integrated health programs, we speak in schools and in rural clinics, sharing the gospel with the people of Chile and forming house churches from those who decide to follow Jesus.

Each town is different. Every person is different. We cannot reach the people with a cookie-cutter strategy. So we are constantly listening and learning and looking for the best methods to use in each community. We must constantly refine our vision as we see what God is doing in the lives of communities, families, and individuals. By doing that we have seen much fruit, fruit that we hope will reproduce many times over, even if we are no longer able to be here. God continues to search our hearts to know our anxious thoughts and continues to lead us on His everlasting way.

∼

Religious Barriers

Loving with God's heart will call us to reach across religious barriers to show His love. Miriam Adeney speaks of Muslim women and the aspects of their faith that have blessed her life, such as their high view of God, their prayer lives, their commitment to community, the expression of their faith publicly, and their ethics. She has come to this appreciation through the relationships she has built with Muslim women.

My friend Laura Savage has been intentional in reaching across religious barriers. While she was working on her master's degree in women's studies at a secular university, she had the opportunity to be around non-Christians each class period. Some of the books the class was asked to read were things she would never have chosen. However, she knew that God had called her to that world, so she sought to read things with a compassionate heart for the authors.

Laura also had to be willing to listen to classmates' opinions and viewpoints that were very different from her own. She learned, though, that if she courteously listened to them, then she could expect them to courteously listen to her. She did not have to try to convince anyone of her view; she simply shared a Christian view when the opportunity arose.

> *For God's purposes to be fulfilled, we all must cross barriers that keep us from going to those who need to be blessed.*

One of the most surprising opportunities came when one of her Muslim classmates invited her to speak to the Introduction to Women's Studies classes she was teaching. She told Laura that she had been listening to the things Laura was saying in their classes together, and she thought her students needed to hear what Laura had to say. Laura had an open door to tell two groups of students in a secular university classroom about the ministries of the Christian organization where she served, all because she was in the same class with her Muslim friend. Once again, God had reminded her that reaching across a religious barrier to build a relationship is a valuable way to have the opportunity to share with them about the most important relationship.

Laura has been intentional in showing God's love through her classes. God's love has set her apart. She will tell you that it was and is God's love that opens doors and transforms lives.

Cultural Barriers

Loving with God's heart will be essential as we continue to see growing numbers of refugees and immigrants crossing our borders. These strangers from "outside" have different languages, religions, foods, and customs. Even those who speak the same language or follow the same religion have great diversity. And within every group are individuals, each of whom God created with a unique personality and unique skills, and each with a divine plan for their lives. Communicating the love of God begins when we show appreciation for the diversity of persons around us by reaching out and becoming a friend.

Diversity continues to challenge the American culture. Throughout America's history, immigrants were expected to decrease their diverse characteristics as they became more "American." In American churches today we often do the same thing, expecting people of varying backgrounds, when they join our fellowship, to become more like us. Instead of expecting new Christians to be transformed by the gospel, we often expect them to be transformed by suburban American Christianity.

Dawson Memorial Baptist Church in Birmingham, Alabama, made an intentional decision ten years ago to reach the Hispanic community in a greater way. The church already had an extensive ministry to internationals, along with an Arabic congregation. As a result of this new decision, they brought a young pastor and his family from Ecuador to lead in the development of the Hispanic ministry.

While the growth of the Hispanic population was expected, little did the members of Dawson realize Birmingham was on the front edge of a huge movement of Hispanics into the community. The amazing growth of the Hispanic congregation is a celebration of the intentional decision of Dawson to find a way to remove the language and culture barriers that kept the church from being as effective as it could be, and from fulfilling its mission as a church. Dawson chooses to do this because they are a congregation seeking to love with God's heart.

Cultural issues are not only concerned with racial or

religious differences but also include such barriers as age, education, and social status. These issues are significant because our country includes many people with limited education, with "rough" jobs and social manners, with less refinement than many middle-class churchgoing people expect in personal relationships. American churches have manufactured many layers of social barriers that can be stumbling blocks to people seeking spiritual truth.

Communicating the love of God begins when we show appreciation for the diversity of persons around us by reaching out and becoming a friend.

In her book *A Beginner's Guide to Crossing Cultures*, Patty Lane tells of teaching a seminar on cross-cultural conflict resolution in which she mentioned that she had not had formal training in this area. Afterward, a participant asked what she had been studying that enabled her to provide such practical and helpful content. She blurted out, "The Bible and the life of Jesus." In response, with an amazed look on his face, the participant said, "Well, you have given me a reason to read one [a Bible]."

Christian families and congregations have a model for intentional relationships in the life of Jesus Christ—a model that is found in no other. Our words, our actions, our teaching, and the way that we live are how we show others who Jesus is and how Jesus loves.

Loving like Jesus results in giving of whatever resources we have at hand, laying down one's life to reach across any and all obstacles to redeem life and soul, with the ultimate goal that God will be glorified and Jesus Christ lifted up. The gospel, the good news of Jesus Christ, is at its core a message of love and acceptance. Those who come to know the love of Jesus become partners in the mission of God to share this love with others.

POLITICAL BARRIERS

Loving with God's heart can also challenge the way we view and respond to the political issues in our country and around the world. Love requires that we embrace people with God's love regardless of their political affiliation.

I met Cathy Bollart at a conference on reconciliation. Her depth of commitment was powerful, and her courage to speak against injustice transformed those who heard her speak. She was singularly focused, intentional in every aspect regarding crossing racial, political, cultural, and religious barriers for the cause of the gospel. Here is her story.

∾

CATHY'S STORY

Coming to Palestine was both a shocking and deeply moving experience. You see, I grew up as a white South African who lived a comfortable, white, and privileged life, quite ignorant of the apartheid regime and the impact it was having on the "other" South Africans. As my quest for truth deepened, my life began to change, as no longer did my reality and belief system line up. Through various experiences, I began to understand a little of what apartheid was about and the dire consequences it had, and continues to have, on both the oppressed and the oppressor. Even though the whites held the power, what we didn't realize is that we were also the victims of our own evil. Fear, greed, power, and religion blinded us to the truth.

Being in Palestine and partially experiencing their reality reminded me too much about the consequences of apartheid in South Africa. It made me realize that if South Africa were Israel, I would have been born an Israeli. If we are to be people of integrity, practicing the lessons and principles we should have learned from our own life and experiences, we must take this issue seriously.

It is not only about the structures, like the checkpoints, the occupation, the house demolitions, and the apartheid wall; it is about what this does to a person, a family, a community, and ultimately to humanity. Having one's house destroyed three times is terrible, but what is even worse is the family that is destroyed through it.

During the TRC (Truth and Reconciliation Commission), many people and churches confessed to the sin of silence, declaring: "We are sorry. We should have done more!" In many ways, "sorry" is too late. We as whites should know better than anybody that to know or to choose not to know and to keep silent is only adding fuel to the fire and giving license for the evil regimes to continue. We should have learned that if we are not a part of the solution, then we are a part of the problem.

What never ceases to amaze me, both in South Africa and in my short Palestinian experience, is the magnanimity of the people who have suffered and been tortured most. Despite their circumstances, they are the ones who know what real life, joy, and peace is all about. I believe it is also true of the people of Palestine. Thanks for teaching me more about what really matters!

BARRIERS JESUS CROSSED
What People Think
Jesus' only concern was to please His Father. He was God's love come to earth. In every decision, every action, He was God's love brought to life. No wonder He was

able to transform lives!

Jesus made His intention clear, even to His earthly family, that He would please God regardless of what others thought. As a child He stayed in the Temple listening to, learning from, and even arguing with the teachers. When his mother chastised Him for worrying them, He answered, "'Why were you searching for me? Did you not know that I must be in my Father's house?'" (Luke 2:49). When his mother wanted him to provide wine at a wedding, Jesus answered, "'Woman, what concern is that to you and to me? My hour has not yet come'" (John 2:4).

As an adult, Jesus acted out of His desire to please God rather than people. Jesus didn't hesitate to accept the gift of worship from a woman known to the Pharisees as "a sinner." She bathed Jesus' feet with her tears and wiped His feet with her hair. In gratitude she kissed and anointed His feet with ointment.

When Jesus saw the abuse of the poor in the temple, He ran the "robbers" out, knowing He would make enemies. Scripture tells us that this event contributed to the desire of the chief priests and scribes to kill Him.

Changing our lifestyles can be difficult when we fear rejection. A nagging voice causes us to be more concerned with the response of our family and friends than we are with God's reaction. Jesus showed us that what others think should not deter us from loving with God's heart.

What People Consider Unclean

Jesus modeled loving the unclean when a woman touched Him. Her desperation gave her courage to touch the bottom of His cloak, hoping that her touch would bring healing from the sickness that had plagued her for years. When Jesus turned and addressed her, she fell down before Him with fear and trembling, expecting the same rejection she had experienced from others. But Jesus responded to her need with loving attention. He spoke to her, affirmed her faith, and rewarded her with complete wholeness. God's love poured out on her through the actions of Jesus.

The "unclean" in our American sphere are often the elderly, the physically and mentally challenged, the sick, and the poor. The book *City of Joy* by Dominique Lapierre tells the story of people who dared to reach across barriers to provide help and hope in the City of Joy, a slum on the edge of Calcutta. When their ministry extended to lepers, others in the community became violent because of their prejudice, hatred, and fear. Lepers had been carefully segregated from the rest of the community; and when they tried to enter into society, they would be persecuted or killed. And those who would dare to embrace them or invite them into their homes and lives would experience the same kind of treatment.

Loving with God's heart brings people together to see what God can do in the most challenging situations.

One church in the city where I live offers the Hearts and Hands Ministry for special-needs adults and children. The Happy Singers is a choir for special-needs adults. One ministry that is provided is a "buddy" system that pairs a special-needs child with a volunteer during Sunday School and worship, allowing the child to be involved in his or her age group or developmentally appropriate environment.

Loving with God's heart is a joyful embracing that brings people together to see what God can do in the most challenging situations.

What People Have Devalued

God's love also embraces women. Women in the first century were viewed like property, yet the Lord of lords counted women among His closest friends. Jesus accepted women who reached out to worship Him. He invited women to sit under His teaching. Women traveled with Him. He drew attention to women who modeled commitment to God. He forgave women and healed women. He appeared to women after His resurrection and commanded women to carry the message of His resurrection to His disciples.

It has been my privilege to lead teams of women around the world as missions volunteers. There has been no end to their capabilities, their commitment, and their boldness in confessing Christ. After returning from the volunteer missions trip to Athens, our team was pleased to receive these words from the Greek Evangelical pastor with whom we worked.

Your team was really a gift from God to us. You left a very strong impression to all of us and especially to the ladies of our church, who were encouraged to take on new initiatives. Many things were very astonishing about your group. First of all, although you were coming from different states and you did not know each other before, there was a sense of unity in the group. Although you had among you all ages from teenagers to grandmothers, there was no tension, but a creative dynamic. I felt the reason for these things was that your ladies were profoundly spiritual and your leadership was admirably wise and gifted.

We were blessed by your humble spirit of service within the church and in the open-air ministry. Your people served as examples of volunteers in a short mission with their willingness to do everything we were asking with the best attitude: you gave out bottles of water under the hot sun, you distributed tracts in a not-so-friendly-to-evangelicals environment, you cleaned up venues, you did face painting and balloon sculpturing, and you supported the Scottish puppet team so beautifully. . . . Is this little? Well, you did more than anybody else and you did all that in the most "Christlike" way!

Leaving our comfort zone to intentionally build relationships can be one of the greatest blessings of all. When the Lord brought down the Tower of Babel, He had much more in mind than punishment. He created the peoples of the world, with unique languages, cultures, and places to live. "The LORD scattered them abroad over the face of all the earth" (Genesis 11:9). But He never stopped loving them, and He never excused them from loving one another. We must make the intentional decision to love with God's heart.

Loving with God's Heart

Barriers in many forms can keep us from loving with God's heart. Jesus told the story of someone who gave a great dinner. When all of the invited guests rejected the invitation, the host told his servant to invite "the poor, the crippled, the blind, and the lame" as well as the people on the roads and lanes. These were the ones who seldom receive an invitation; and, most likely, their appreciation was far greater than it would have been from those first invited.

The Lord has left us in charge of the banquet. Who will be seated at our table? What barriers will we cross to intentionally love with God's heart?

TELLING GOD'S STORY:

Communicating Christ

*W*hen I came to you, brothers and sisters, I did not come proclaiming the mystery of God to you in lofty words or wisdom. For I decided to know nothing among you except Jesus Christ, and him crucified. And I came to you in weakness and in fear and in much trembling. My speech and my proclamation were not with plausible words of wisdom, but with demonstration of the Spirit and of power, so that your faith might rest not on human wisdom but on the power of God.

—1 Corinthians 2:1–5

TELLING GOD'S STORY

Commitment to a lifestyle based on gospel weapons of witness and love are revolutionary, in that they are in complete contrast with the world.
—Stanley Hauerwas and William H. Willimon, *Resident Aliens*

The worship team was rehearsing in the sanctuary. When I came in to listen, one of the singers introduced herself and began to tell me about her life. She spoke of wanting to be the next Madonna, but having her dreams dashed when she discovered she was pregnant. Then she and her boyfriend encountered God's love in Christ and their lives were transformed. Now, she is happily married and the mother of one and foster mother of five. She is singing for God and telling His story.

God's story is a love story. "God shows me His love through you." These words on a little framed print, a gift from a friend, tell God's story. God has been showing His love from the beginning. The Bible is the recorded story of God making His love known. The ultimate gesture of God in making His love known was to stoop down from heaven to save us, sending His Son Jesus in human form, so God's love could walk among the people. Jesus showed us God's love in the way He lived. Then He showed us God's love by dying for our sins on a cross. And finally, He showed us God's love by rising from the grave, conquering death for all time.

Jesus explained God's story to Nicodemus one night. "'For God so loved the world that he gave his only Son, so that everyone who believes in him may not perish but may have eternal life. Indeed, God did not send the Son into the world to condemn the world, but in order that the world might be saved through him. Those who believe in him are not condemned; but those who do not believe are condemned already, because they have not believed in the name of the only Son of God'" (John 3:16–18).

Jesus helped Nicodemus understand that God's love was revealed in Jesus and was available to all who would accept it. He also explained that to reject Jesus was to reject God, for God has chosen to make His love known through His Son.

Telling God's story begins with trusting in God's Son, Jesus. Until we accept God's Son, we cannot tell God's story; for God's story is only revealed through Jesus. Telling God's story begins with our personal response to God's love. Just as Christ was the incarnation of God's love, we become the incarnation of Christ in the world, proclaiming Christ through who we are, what we do, and what we say. Through us God's love is lived out for the world to see. Second Corinthians 2:14 beautifully describes this incarnation of God's love as "the fragrance that comes from knowing him." Telling God's story is an evangelism that comes from the heart, and from a clear understanding that people can only know God's love through Christ.

Until we accept God's Son, we cannot tell God's story; for God's story is only revealed through Jesus.

Telling God's story is the privilege and accountability of any who know God's story. In fact, when we truly understand what God has done for us in Christ, we can't keep from telling His story. His story will overflow in the way we live and in our words. We want others to know about God's love!

How long has it been since you overflowed with the love of God so that you could not contain the good news of Jesus? My friend Laura knows God's love, and is so filled with His love that she has made an intentional commitment to tell God's story through her life, her relationships, and her words. Recently she shared one way she is involved in intentional evangelism.

~

LAURA'S STORY

For more than a year, I've been living the adventure of a lifetime as an academic missionary in a foreign country. God has blessed me with wonderful relationships with young female university students. One of the reasons those relationships have developed is because I opened my home to my students. I invited them over to watch videos for class and then we would discuss them—over snacks, of course.

I opened my life to them as well. Being single allows me the freedom to spend time with them, going shopping, having them over for pizza, talking about guys and dating, and talking about my life in the US, including my Christian upbringing and my personal relationship with Jesus. I don't have to push the gospel, I just talk about my experience, and that causes them to ask questions.

The greatest joy was when three of them asked me to lead them in a weekly Bible study. These young women have a deep hunger for spiritual things—more than they realize. We read a portion of Scripture and talk about what it means. This is the first time they have ever been encouraged to read the Bible for themselves. One of them has no church background of any kind. Another one has a strong religious background, but no real understanding of a personal faith. And the other one has some religious knowledge, but is simply curious and searching. Their fresh insights have enlightened me on some stories that are all too familiar, reminding me of the infinite truths that God's Word offers.

One day, one of these young women told me about her own childhood and early teen years. Her mother left her with her grandparents when she was an infant and she has only heard from her mother once in the last 23 years. She also confessed that she tried to commit suicide when she was in eighth grade. Her upbringing by her grandparents seems to have been more about tolerance than love and encouragement.

I know that God has brought me halfway around the world to love this young woman like no one has ever loved her before. She finds a reason to come by my apartment every day. We share a meal. She uses my computer. We talk about her favorite rock band. I tell her I love her and I try to drop in spiritual reasons for the way I do and don't do certain things. She is like a daughter to me. I can't imagine my life without her now. I'm praying that I will hear her pray to receive Christ someday—but even if I don't, I know God has called me to love her, just like God first loved me.

Communicating God's love to others is best done when you can look into their eyes, hold their hands, put an arm around their shoulders, taste their tears, listen to their stories, and feel their joys and their pains—because only then will they smell the aroma of Christ. That's why Jesus said, "Go!"

~

INTENTIONALLY AUTHENTIC

Laura's story is a beautiful illustration of true evangelism. The Lausanne Covenant is a statement adopted in 1974 by a group of Christians from around the world at the

International Congress on World Evangelization; this covenant encourages believers to be creative and pioneering in finding ways to share God's story through our life and words. The covenant says that evangelism is "to spread the good news that Jesus Christ died for our sin and was raised from the dead according to the Scriptures, and that as the reigning Lord he now offers the forgiveness of sins and the liberating gifts of the Spirit to all who repent and believe"; but the covenant also warns us to not confuse our *culture* with the gospel. The description goes on to say that evangelism seeks to persuade "people to come to him personally and so be reconciled to God."

> *Our commitment to prayer and Bible study allows God to open our minds to the truths of the gospel.*

Our commitment to prayer and Bible study allows God to open our minds to the truths of the gospel. In this way we learn to differentiate the gospel from the practices and traditions that, in truth, have little to do with Christian faith and practice. When we convert people to our culture rather than to Christ, we are leaving them empty of hope. In his book *Transforming Mission*, David Bosch warns that only as we bring people to the "Christ of the gospels" are we practicing authentic evangelism.

Jesus gave an example of authentic evangelism when He spoke to a Samaritan woman near Sychar in Samaria. Though He was a Jew who perfectly followed God's law, Jesus did not ask the woman to leave her people or become a Jew. Instead, He explained to her that God was not confined to a people or a place, but that He is worshipped in spirit and in truth, "'for the Father seeks such as these to worship him. God is spirit, and those who worship him must worship in spirit and truth'" (John 4:23–24).

The Aboriginal people of Australia tell the story of

those who came in the name of Christ and demanded that they give up their culture, their music, and their families to become Christians. Many Aborigine babies were taken out of their homes and put in the homes of white families so they could become "Christian."

David Bosch explains that authentic evangelism is about "liberating people from themselves, their sins, and their entanglements, so that they will be free for God and neighbor. It calls individuals to a life of openness, vulnerability, wholeness, and love. To win people to Jesus is to win their allegiance to God's priorities." Such evangelism will result in cultures being influenced not by other cultures but by God's love.

In other words, evangelism is more than telling someone about Jesus, and evangelism is not taking people out of their biological culture group. True evangelism is about introducing people to a new reason for living and a new way of living—in Christ. It is about introducing people to Jesus, not our culture. Evangelism is investing ourselves in another person to the extent that they are able to leave their old life behind for the new life that God offers. When the woman at the well met Jesus, she left her old life at the well and went back to her city to tell the people, "'Come and see a man who told me everything I have ever done! He cannot be the Messiah, can he?'" (John 4:29). She already knew the answer, and her testimony caused many to believe. She did not leave her culture, but there is no doubt her encounter with Jesus changed her and changed the city she lived in.

SonRise Church in Ocean Pines, Maryland, has made an intentional effort to be authentic in their evangelism. They accept people just as they are and allow the love of God in Christ to do the transformation. They have seen people not only come to Christ, but also be freed from alcoholism, drug abuse, depression, and marital problems. One Sunday morning when I was visiting the church, a commercial fisherman gave his testimony of being freed from cursing. When people come to Christ, they are freed from the past to a new worldview. The cursing that previously seemed right becomes uncomfortable—old sinful habits don't "fit" our lives anymore. Just like this fisherman, we begin to see the world through God's eyes.

The congregation of SonRise is telling God's story. They are investing all they are and all they have into something that God is already doing in their midst. Their ministries, their activities, where and when they meet, their work and their friendships, and their involvement in their community make Christ accessible.

One week I was honored to spend some time getting to know this group of believers. Again and again they told of persons in the church who had influenced them to Christ through their love, joy, and service. While pastor Daryl McCready and I were involved in the Good Friday activities of the community, secretary Terri Budd was at the church office (not in a church, but in an office building). She had been praying about leading someone to Christ, and God answered her prayer. I think you will be encouraged by her story.

~

TERRI'S STORY

Pastor Daryl and I were to escort Andrea to Ocean City for the Good Friday service. The rest of the week had been so hectic that I knew I needed to stay behind and get my work done. I felt bad because I really wanted to go to the service. After they left, Jenna came by my office.

Our family and the church had been praying for Jenna to accept Christ. We had invited her to church on many occasions and she would accept and come with us. But each time the event or service was over, she would leave without having made a decision. We were crushed, not knowing what would reach her. We loved her so very much and wanted her to know Christ and accept Him into her life.

That Friday, when Jenna came to the office, I knew that she was having some difficulties in a relationship. I saw her car pull into the driveway and prayed for God to give me the right words to say to her, especially since I didn't know why she was coming to see me.

It turned out that she came by to see if I could give her a phone number of a friend of our family from church. After I gave her the phone number, she was saying good-bye and turning to walk out. I could see that she was on the verge of tears, so I asked her to let me give her a hug before she left.

I opened my mouth, and I know the words must have come straight from God. I told her how I didn't know what would help in her relationship but I knew what would help in her life. I explained to her about the void or hole that is empty within, waiting to be filled, and how nothing can ever satisfy that void other than Jesus. I explained to her very carefully how God loves us.

A few weeks earlier, Jenna had seen the movie *The Passion of the Christ*. I explained how Christ suffered all of that because He loved her. I explained how Jesus knocks on the door to your heart, but the doorknob is only on the inside and He would never barge His way into someone's life. He would enter if He was invited.

We continued to talk about what may be holding her back from making a decision. She explained her reasons . . . she hadn't been ready and didn't understand. I finally asked her if there was any reason now that she would not want to accept Jesus at this moment. And she said, "No, there is no reason." There was nothing holding her back. She was ready to accept Him into her heart and life, and we prayed together right there in my office.

We cried together and were excited to tell family and friends of her decision to accept Christ. It was exciting to be able to tell Pastor Daryl that she had accepted Christ when he and Andrea returned from the Good Friday service.

Since that time, Jenna and I remain very close. I spent some time mentoring her and going through a study with her. She has since gone through our new believer's class. She was baptized by Pastor Daryl and faithfully attends SonRise Church.

I have never in my life been so blessed as when I was given the opportunity to lead this precious young lady to the Lord.

~

God's Work

Terri would be the first to say that what happened in Jenna's life is something that only God could do. Winning persons to Christ is God's work. David F. Wells explains in his book *Turning to God* that Christian conversion is a supernatural encounter with God through His Son Jesus Christ. "Without God's saving action in Christ, conversion would not be possible. Without the convincing work of the Holy Spirit, conversion would not be desirable." Conversion is the supernatural work of God's grace. Coming to Christ is unlike any other conversion. It isn't just making a mental decision to live in a new way. It is not only giving up a bad habit or deciding to attend church. Christian conversion is initiated by God and accomplished by God.

He destined us for adoption as his children through Jesus Christ, according to the good pleasure of his will, to the praise of his glorious grace that he freely bestowed on us in the Beloved.

—Ephesians 1:5

Conversion is what God does through Jesus to bring us into God's family for all eternity, and there is no human means by which we can do what only God can do. It is the Holy Spirit who convicts of sin and who reveals who Christ is. It is a divine grace gift from God.

LED BY THE HOLY SPIRIT

So, obviously, all our arguments, words, and actions are useless apart from the Holy Spirit working through us. As Jerry Wiles explains in *How to Win Others to Christ*, "Soul winning is putting yourself in a position for the Holy Spirit to win souls through what He prompts you to say and do." How do we put ourselves in the right position to be used? I think of four ways that Wiles mentions to be in the position.

1. Be in relationship with God through prayer, Bible study, and obedience. You'll be ready with the right heart and attitude, and you will experience the Spirit guiding you.

2. Be where people do not know Christ. This may be in your own home, next door, or where you shop and work.

3. Be ready to tell how Jesus is relevant to your life. Bring the name of Jesus into the conversation. Tell of your personal relationship with Him and how He makes a difference in your everyday life.

4. Be ready to help others come to Christ. Help them to know that they can have what you have.

Jerry Wiles reminds us that our part is to respond to the prompting of the Holy Spirit and allow God to do what only He can do. God wants to use us to accomplish His work. Darrell L. Guder writes in *The Continuing Conversion of the Church*, "The New Testament activity defined as 'evangelizing' and 'evangelization' focused on the communication of the gospel so that people might respond and become followers of Jesus Christ." The Holy Spirit will lead us to be evangelists, and the more we experience His leadership, the more we will want to tell the good news of Jesus Christ not only through our lives but through our words.

> *The more we experience the Holy Spirit's leadership, the more we will want to tell the good news of Jesus Christ.*

Scripture supports the fact that we have an important role in sharing the gospel. "So we are ambassadors for Christ, since God is making his appeal through us: we entreat you on behalf of Christ, be reconciled to God" (2 Corinthians 5:20). The Apostle Paul asked, "But how are they to call on one in whom they have not believed? And how are they to believe in one of whom they have never heard? And how are they to hear without someone to proclaim him? And how are they to proclaim him unless they are sent? As it is written, 'How beautiful are the feet of those who bring good news!'" (Romans 10:14–15).

The New Testament church understood their vocation as being witnesses to Christ. They were eyewitnesses to the life of Jesus and passed on the good news of Jesus' life, death, and resurrection. "Although the predominant meaning of witness has to do with oral communication, there is ample reason to understand witness in a much more comprehensive sense, as defining the entire life, both individually and corporately," explains Darrell

Guder. Being a living witness certainly depends on the presence and filling of the Holy Spirit. This is the prerequisite for telling God's story through the way you live.

BEING CHRIST

Telling God's story includes proclaiming and bringing the good news. But effective storytelling involves far more than speaking words. In his book *Transforming Mission*, David Bosch explains that communicating the gospel means "mediating the good news of God's love in Christ that transforms life, proclaiming, by word and action, that Christ has set us free." In other words, to explore *intentional* communication of the gospel, we must look at more than just our verbal witness.

Telling God's story begins with who we are. Acts 1:8 tells us, "You will be my witnesses"—it doesn't just say "do witnessing." When we realize that who we are is the primary witness to Christ, we see that becoming like Christ is of the utmost importance. Are people seeing the true Christ in us?

Enabling people to see Christ in our lives calls us to be unique in the ways that we respond to life's situations. The story of Paul and Silas is a good illustration of this. They were thrown in prison for freeing a slave girl from demonic control. Rather than responding with hysterical fear or debilitating hatred, Scripture tells us they "were praying and singing hymns to God, and the prisoners were listening to them" (Acts 16:25). While they were singing and praying, an earthquake shook the prison, the prison doors were opened, and the chains fell off all the prisoners!

Amazingly, none of the prisoners left. When the jailer awoke and discovered the situation, he assumed all had fled and was going to kill himself. Then Paul shouted to him, "'Do not harm yourself, for we are all here'" (Acts 16:28).

The astounded jailer asked how he might be saved, giving Paul and Silas an opportunity to tell him and his family about Jesus, and bring all of them to salvation.

The behaviors of Paul and Silas reflected Christ's love. Had they and the other prisoners fled, this jailer would have killed himself, and neither he nor any of his family would have come to Christ. The worship of God through the praying and singing of praise prepared Paul and Silas for the opportunity that was about to come. They weren't afraid to remain in the prison once the doors were opened, for they knew exactly whose care they were in. They had nothing to fear from jailers or governments. They knew they were safely in the hands of God.

> *As people watch us go about the living out of our lives, they are either drawn to Christ or turned away.*

Whether the jailer's question to Paul was for physical or spiritual salvation, he recognized a power at work far beyond human understanding. He saw something in Paul and Silas that caused him to know they had the key to his salvation. As people watch us go about the living out of our lives, they are either drawn to Christ or turned away. Intentional evangelism begins long before the name of Jesus is spoken to another person. It begins with an awareness throughout each day that the way we treat others, the decisions we make, and the things we do are elements of our evangelistic influence.

BUILDING BRIDGES

Paul and Silas built a bridge to the jailer through their actions. Telling God's story means building bridges. To do this, we must be willing to listen to others. In *How Will They Hear If We Don't Listen?* Ron Wilson suggests that we seek to have a conversation rather than make a presentation. In this way the other person is valued and the truth of Christ is personalized for the individual. Jesus gave us the example of speaking to people with stories and illustrations they could understand. Jesus comes to us within our culture and changes us so that we change the world around us. Jesus appreciated people's history. He affirmed who they were, where they had come from, and what they did.

Sometimes those to whom we are building bridges are "outsiders," or persons whose experience with Christianity is from outside the Christian faith. In other words, their homes contain no Christian teaching. Their society may have no Christian influence. For Jews and Muslims, Christianity is often seen as a force of opposition to their very identity. Hindus believe God is manifested in many ways, and Buddhists consider spiritual conversion to be the freeing of the mind from the illusion of the physical world and all its concerns. Building bridges to these groups, as with others whose thought and religious practice is threatened by or opposite of Christian belief, can be rewarding as we learn to appreciate those aspects of faith that these groups value, while at the same time practicing before them our relationship with God and the love and hope we have in Jesus Christ.

Steve Sjogren writes in *Conspiracy of Kindness* of the power of kindness in building bridges. Kindness is offering to do something for another person in humble service with no strings attached. Such kindness paints a picture of the grace of God. Kindness is seen in deeds of love. When asked why we serve, we respond with words of love rather than a canned presentation. We then give adequate time for the Holy Spirit to use the deeds and words of love to soften hearts and open minds.

INTENTIONAL IN LIFESTYLE, DEED, AND WORD

Intentional communication involves lifestyle, deed, and word. David Bosch, in summarizing evangelism, provides an excellent definition of intentional evangelism in its fullest form.

> *That dimension and activity of the church's mission which, by word and deed and in the light of particular conditions and particular context, offers every person and community, everywhere, a valid opportunity to be directly challenged to a radical reorientation of their lives, a reorientation which involves such things as deliverance from slavery to the world and its powers; embracing Christ as Savior and Lord; becoming a living member of his community, the church; being enlisted into his service of reconciliation, peace, and justice on earth; and being committed to God's purpose of placing all things under the rule of Christ.*

Lifestyles that imitate Jesus are intentionally committed to communicating the gospel in ways that transform lives and societies. Deeds that come from hearts moved with compassion communicate. As for words, Jerry Wiles writes, "I believe the early Church was so full of Christ and so full of the Spirit—they had believed and received so much—that their hearts were literally bubbling over with the Lord. They had such a flow of joy and peace and inner reality within them that they couldn't contain it. That which was inside them overflowed into their every conversation." Jesus said, "Let the one who believes in me drink. As the scripture has said, 'Out of the believer's heart shall flow rivers of living water'" (John 7:38).

Speaking the Name of Jesus

Every time I talk with another person about coming to Christ, the conversation is unique. But the message is always the same, for the gospel, the good news, doesn't change: "that Christ died for our sins in accordance with the scriptures, and that he was buried, and that he was raised on the third day in accordance with the scriptures" (1 Corinthians 15:3–4).

Jesus is the good news! Four points, easy to remember, offer a simple approach to telling God's story to your friends, neighbors, or someone you meet in a brief encounter.

1. God loves us (John 3:16)
2. Our sin has separated us from God. (Romans 6:23)
3. God sent His Son to die for our sins. (Romans 5:8; 4:24–25)
4. When we accept Christ's sacrifice, God gifts us with eternal life. (John 3:16)

As you share these four points, you will be able to point to God as the only God, as the God who created us and sustains us. You can tell the story of how sin came into the world and what sin is. You can tell about God's plan to restore our relationship with Him. You can then tell about Jesus, God's Son, and His voluntary payment on our behalf. Give the good news that God offers us a new life right now, and eternal life with Him.

At some point, we must speak the good news! The more often we bring the name of Jesus into our conversation, the more natural it will become. "Evangelism does have an inescapable verbal dimension. In a society marked by relativism and agnosticism it is necessary to name the Name of the One in whom we believe," David Bosch urges.

People who are hungry to hear surround us. We find

it hard to believe this is true, but when we begin to bring Jesus into our conversation, we discover that God is already there working. Yes, people are waiting for us to bring the good news! They are waiting for us to be intentional about telling God's story, the greatest story ever told.

Telling God's Story
Jesus is the sweetest name I know. What about you? If you agree, how will you become intentional in telling God's story wherever you are?

SERVING WITH GOD'S STRENGTH:
Ministry

*T*hen the king will say to those at his right hand,
"Come, you that are blessed by my Father, inherit the
kingdom prepared for you from the foundation of the
world; for I was hungry and you gave me food, I was thirsty and
you gave me something to drink, I was a stranger and you welcomed me, I was naked and you gave me clothing, I was sick and
you took care of me, I was in prison and you visited me."

—Matthew 25:34–36

Serving with God's Strength

As we minister, we make our own wounds available, as a source of healing.

—Ann Platz, *The Best Is Yet to Come*

CNN covered the tsunami that hit several Asian countries in December 2004. When the United States was accused of giving limited help, an early morning CNN news show asked people to email them with their opinion about how America should respond. News correspondents were surprised to see how many respondents felt that Americans should take care of Americans first.

Even believers are confused about service. When CNN's talk show host, Larry King, invited religious leaders from many diverse traditions to discuss the tsunami, where God was in this human tragedy, and how we should respond, the presenter from one evangelical denomination failed to express God's concern for the physical and emotional needs of people. His lack of understanding regarding the Jesus who walked among the people with great compassion, who revealed His compassion by meeting not only spiritual needs but physical needs, was evident.

No doubt, caring about others deeply means that we must invest our lives and resources in others. It calls for a love that frees us to give ourselves away. Caring enough to change our attitudes and overcome our fears is uncommon apart from God. We hesitate to step out of our comfort zone to minister to the needs of those in the hardest places. But when we do, we find that the ministry God calls us to is the greatest of all blessings.

Serving with God's strength is a call for *agape* love; this is the steadfast, unwavering love of God toward us and toward all people. If we regard a person with agape, it means that nothing he can do will make us seek anything but his highest good—even if that person doesn't like us, and even if that person is himself "unlikable." Our agape love for someone is not dependent on what that person does.

Love like this can only come through God's strength. We choose to let God work through us to sustain our love toward the unlovely and the unlovable. In John 4, Jesus and His disciples traveled through Samaria en route to Galilee, even though Jews at that time would go out of their way not to enter Samaria. Jesus chose to go through Samaria, not because of convenience, not because it was the comfortable, acceptable, and safe place to be, but because of the compelling love of God for all peoples. Jesus perceived ministry to be not only with His own people, but with any people in need of help.

It is only in God's strength that we are able to act with mercy toward all people.

When Jesus went to Matthew's house and sat with tax collectors and sinners, He was criticized. Religious leaders thought He should only go to those who were acceptable, who were among the "approved." But Jesus said to His followers, "'Those who are well have no need of a physician, but those who are sick. Go and learn what this means, "I desire mercy, not sacrifice." For I have come to call not the righteous but sinners'" (Matthew 9:12–13).

From the beginning Jesus showed that it is only in God's strength that we are able to act with mercy toward all people. In God's strength, Jesus demolished structures to meet human need. Jesus' dependence on God's strength enabled Him to walk right over political, cultural, and religious barriers to touch, heal, feed, restore, forgive, guide, and love the discouraged, distressed, lonely, feeble, and forgotten.

THE HUMAN COMMUNITY

Serving with God's strength revolutionizes our understanding of community, for God's love extends to all people in all places. Where once we were exclusive, now we are inclusive, welcoming the world into our understanding of community. We move beyond concern for status to a new accountability for our neighbor.

A primary religious group in a small town where I lived for many years had a practice of caring only for their own people. When indigent people would come to town in need of help, the local police would instead call our little church, for they knew that our pastor and our congregation would meet whatever need we could. As a result, our pastor was named Most Valuable Citizen several years in a row.

When God's strength is the lens of life through which we view every person in every situation, we respond differently to tsunamis in distant places or indigent travelers in our own town. The take-care-of-me-and-mine-first attitude becomes instead, "I must do all I can, seeking God's strength to do more than I can do on my own." God's strength places in our hearts a passion to give all we can to help those around us and those in faraway places.

Often it takes a tsunami to open people's hearts to the needs of others, but for believers in Christ, who serve with God's strength, love and mercy should be an automatic response to the smallest need. Serving with God's strength results in our giving whatever we can to help, whether it be a touch, a check, our time, or all three.

God doesn't call us to respond out of our limited human reservoir. Our service is all about God's strength, not our own. Every gift, every ability we have for service comes from God. God is the giver, the equipper, the strengthener for whatever He calls us to do.

NEW LIFE GIFTS FOR SERVICE

My grandson Nicolas is too young to understand "serving with God's strength," but he is not too young to understand that all good gifts come from God. When Nicolas celebrated his seventh birthday, he received Spider-Man gifts from family and friends who know of his interest in this comic book hero now come to movies. These were gifts given as a celebration of Nicolas's seven years of life, and have little value beyond the immediate joy and expression of love they represent. Someday Nicolas will receive the gifts of heaven promised to those who trust in Christ, the very gifts that will equip Nicolas to serve with God's strength.

God always chooses the gifts that will bring us the greatest joy and be of the greatest value.

Paul wrote to the Christians in Rome, "We have gifts . . ." We have gifts that come with the new life we've received in Christ, and those gifts have value for us as well as for those around us. These are gifts given to bless us so that we might serve with God's strength. Paul mentions gifts of prophecy, ministry, teaching, exhorting, giving, leading, and compassion. Paul explains that our gifts are given "according to the measure of faith that God has assigned," and that "we have gifts that differ according to the grace given to us." In other words, our gifts come as a result of Christ in us, not anything we have done ourselves. God is pleased to lavish us with gifts from Him. And because He knows us perfectly, He always chooses the gifts that will bring us the greatest joy and be of the greatest value.

God's gifts do more than bless. They are meant to strengthen us to be blessings to others. Paul explained that these gifts have a resulting ministry attached to them. Prophecy conveys faith. Ministry meets needs. Teaching equips others. Exhorting builds up for the long haul. Giving is generous. Leading charts the way. Compassion lifts and cheers. Gifts build up the body of Christ. Since every gift comes from God, it is obvious that serving is always with God's strength.

Our life in Christ comes with gifts. Our gifts are the outpouring of God's love on us, the blessing that we have been given, through which we are to bless others. Our gifts are a divine anointing from our Father through His Son, Jesus, empowering us to bring transformation wherever our gifts are used.

In my book *Extraordinary Living* I gave some thought to how these gifts become tangible blessings to those around us.

Apostleship can help us risk going beyond familiar environments to meet needs and share Christ with others.

Prophecy allows us to become advocates who guide others toward godly lives.

Teaching brings Bible truths alive in ways that are relevant and applicable to daily life.

Ministry softens a heart to the gospel as a visible sign of God's love to a lost and hurting world.

Evangelism leads others to Christ through both lifestyle and words.

Exhortation supplies what is needed to hold on in faith when the going is rough.

Giving releases abundant resources for kingdom purposes.

Compassion empathizes with another's suffering, relieving pain with caring words and actions.

Help does whatever is needed.

Leadership brings together people with all kinds of gifts to accomplish a common goal.

Wisdom and knowledge work hand in hand to clarify the direction we are to take as we seek to fulfill God's design.

Faith extends ministries in ways that only God can accomplish.

Hospitality makes everyone feel welcome.

Discernment sees beyond words to the heart and mind.

Healing and miracles reveal the supernatural power of God at work in the world.

Tongues and interpretation of tongues is a language of worship that encourages awe before God.

Gifts are just one of the many ways that God blesses us so that we might bless others. He ensures we have everything we need for life and for blessing. He provides His strength for our service. In 2 Peter 1:3–4 we read, "His divine power has given us everything needed for life and godliness, through the knowledge of him who called us by his own glory and goodness. Thus he has given us, through these things, his precious and very great promises, so that through them you may escape from the corruption that is in the world because of lust, and may become participants of the divine nature." Participating in the divine nature is the greatest of all blessings! We are allowed to experience the glory and goodness of God.

Peter continues in this passage to admonish his readers to make every effort to live within the boundaries of goodness, knowledge, self-control, endurance, godliness, mutual affection, and love. He assures us that in living this way we will be effective and fruitful. And we will be richly blessed. "For in this way, entry into the eternal kingdom of our Lord and Savior Jesus Christ will be richly provided for you" (2 Peter 1:11). Serving with God's strength includes the ultimate reward, another gift from God— eternal and abundant life, both right now and forever!

SPIRITUAL BLESSINGS IN SERVICE

Serving with God's strength always leads to our being blessed. After returning from our missions trip to Athens,

Greece, Javee Martinez, one of the collegiate women on my team, shared how God blessed her as she used the gifts God had given to her.

Javee's Story

Walking into a shop while in Athens, Greece, I had a greater purpose than simply shopping for souvenirs and gifts. The purpose was that of sharing Christ and building relationships with those who worked in the shop. God taught me the importance of looking at every person we meet as an opportunity to share Christ. He led me to see that there are many ways that I can share my faith. Until the trip to Athens, I did not know that I could tell others about Jesus so openly, even though I had known them but a few minutes.

From the woman that fixed my coffee every day at Starbucks, to the family that owned the leather shop, to the mom of the children I made balloon animals for, I was blessed and filled with joy by the smiles I saw cross their faces when they heard about the love of Christ. The more I told others about Christ, the more I looked forward to the next opportunity to come. For the first time in my life, I became intentional about sharing my faith and equipping myself to be able to share my faith in many different ways.

As a result of this experience in Greece, God has renewed the passion He has given me for children's ministry. Showing a child God's love always brings joy to my life. My mind is full of memories of children whose lives I touched while in Greece. The smile that crossed the child's face when I made him a balloon animal or the child that thought it was the coolest thing to have his face painted were just small ways in which I saw our ministry to the children come to life.

However, the ministry did not stop with the children. In reaching the children, we were also able to reach the parents. In several situations, we were able to reach the parent by reaching the child. We met one little boy while shopping at the beginning of the week. At the end of the week, I met the boy's family in the store, which they owned. I was able to use that as an opportunity to share Christ with the parents of the boy. Another woman was so pleased by the love we were showing her children that she was open to my sharing Christ with her. Through opportunities like these, God confirmed my passion for ministry to children, and ministering to the families as well.

∾

OUR SERVICE PLANNED BY GOD

Javee illustrates in her story the truth that God has the plan. "For we are what he has made us, created in Christ Jesus for good works, which God prepared beforehand to be our way of life." One of God's foremost blessings to us is our discovery that God truly has a plan for our lives, and serving with God's strength is the living out of God's plan. This is where faith is born, in the discovery place of God's plan. It is in this discovering that we find fulfillment and meaning in life. The "good works" are not just good for others—they are also good for us. This doesn't mean they will always be easy for us to do, or be what we had in mind for ourselves. No, they may be difficult and may require great sacrifice. They may take us far from home or require that we stay where we are. Most certainly, they will disrupt our schedules and call us to act in times that are not convenient and in ways that are not comfortable. They will unbalance us as God uses these good works to help us see the world through His eyes and to learn to love with His heart. Our Lord, because He loves us and because He blesses us, will stretch us and lead us into ministry and service where He alone has the power and wisdom to bring hope, healing, and transformation. His plan will turn us toward Him again and again, as we discover anew that we need Him more and more. Serving with God's strength becomes our way of life.

With God we can open the doors of heaven for those who are in the deepest valleys of sin and sorrow.

Needing and turning to God are the blessings of doing the good works He has planned for us, of serving with His strength. Apart from God we can do nothing of lasting value, but with Him we can open the doors of heaven for those who are in the deepest valleys of sin and sorrow. Whatever God has planned, He is the sole reason for whatever we may do. He is the initiator and the supplier, and in Him alone can any good work accomplish its goal.

Intentional About Service

Developing skills for our unique ministry setting is at the heart of serving with God's strength. God has intentioned each of us toward specific areas of service through the gifts, skills, abilities, and experiences He has placed in our lives.

We are called to serve through many types of ministries, such as working with the homeless, the hungry, the poor, the disabled, the elderly, and others who have significant needs. On the other hand, the needs are also great among those who "have." The needs are perhaps unique, but wealth and possessions do not guarantee that we will not be lonely, rejected, fearful, or sick, or that we will not experience grief, divorce, loss, and most other significant difficulties of life.

The more competent our skills, the greater our potential to make a difference in the lives of those God sends us, whether they are preschoolers, children, youth, or adults, whether they are young or old, rich or poor, in our community or on the far side of the globe. Competency comes as we use our gifts and as we take advantage of the opportunities to learn more about our ministry.

I began to teach children in Sunday School when my daughter was a few years old. The opportunity came to attend a training event in a city about 100 miles away. Because of a serious snowstorm, I was the only student who showed up for the class. At that time, I knew little about teaching children, but through this teacher and others I continued to increase my understanding.

Through the years my ministry has changed as God has led; but in the process of following Him, I have found that His purposes have become more and more central to my life journey. My growing commitment to His purposes has led me to fill roles where someone was needed. Sometimes no one else was available to do the job. I wasn't necessarily the best one for the job, but the task needed to be done.

When you choose to live for God's purposes, you will be willing to do those tasks that are not always at the top of your list of things you want to do. You do them because you are willing to do whatever it takes to see the world come to Christ, and you understand that even the small and sometimes large tasks are important if this is to happen. Perhaps these are the times when you most discover the greatness of God's strength as He works through you to accomplish His purposes.

The decision comes back to whether you are

intentional about serving God. If you are, He will ask you to do those things that need to be done, even when it isn't your ministry passion, and He will ask you to depend on His strength alone.

SERVING WHERE GOD IS WORKING

The tsunami in Asia at the end of 2004 focused the needs of the world on millions of people who had lost family, homes, businesses, jobs, and every earthly possession. In response, within a few days over $1 billion had been pledged from governments and through relief agencies. People from many countries began inquiring about adopting children left without parents and family. Volunteers offered to help in any way that was needed. Medical personnel, construction workers, and others went on-site to provide medical care, cleanup, and rebuilding of lives.

How can we tell where God is at work? Scripture provides some insight that might help us recognize His presence and concern.

• God is at work where people have need. "When the poor and needy seek water, and there is none, and their tongue is parched with thirst, I the Lord will answer them, I the God of Israel will not forsake them" (Isaiah 41:17).
• God is at work where people are oppressed. "I have given you as a covenant to the people, a light to the nations, to open the eyes that are blind, to bring out the prisoners from the dungeon, from the prison those who sit in darkness" (Isaiah 42:6–7).
• God is at work where people need Christ. "Then he opened their minds to understand the scriptures, and he said to them, 'Thus it is written, that the Messiah is to suffer and to rise from the dead on the third day, and that repentance and forgiveness of sins is to be proclaimed in

his name to all nations, beginning from Jerusalem'" (Luke 24:45–47).

• God is at work in every heart, seeking to bring all people to Himself. "Indeed, God did not send the Son into the world to condemn the world, but in order that the world might be saved through him" (John 3:17).

SERVING WITH PASSION

Along with opening our eyes to see God at work around us, we can also open our minds so God can help us discover our passion and where He would have us live out that passion. Rick Warren, in *The Purpose-Driven Life*, suggests that God has given each of us a passion for something so that everything that needs to be done on earth will be accomplished. We can boldly claim the ministry where we find our God-given passion. What is your passion? Are you intentionally focused toward your passion, wherever you are? Listed below are some of the ways God has given His people passion to do His work. What would you add? Are one of these the very thing God would have you do?

• Serving in your home
• Working in your profession
• Going about your daily routines
• Living and working with the poorest of the poor
• Working with women and children in poverty
• Ministering to persons in need of food, clothing, and shelter
• Working with corporate and government leaders
• Running for office or serving on a school board
• Being an advocate for changes in legislation and policies that are unjust
• Encouraging persons experiencing life crises through one-on-one and group experiences
• Working with various age groups in the church

- Working with persons of other languages and culture groups
- Serving refugees and displaced persons
- Teaching in a school or in higher education to bring a Christian worldview
- Leading Bible study groups
- Leading missions volunteer teams
- Developing multifamily housing ministries
- Teaching English as a second language
- Tutoring and helping foster literacy
- Ministering to AIDS patients
- Giving care
- Ministering to the elderly
- Intervening with substance abusers and those whose lives and homes are impacted

In *A Work of Heart*, Reggie McNeal argues that individual believers should be helped to develop a personal sense of mission. "The lack of this among Christians is one of the great tragedies of the modern church. A hopeful sign in more recent years is the recognition by churches of this general calling and the ensuing efforts to intentionally help believers identify their passion and personal servant profiles. Individual believers live out their personal sense of call or mission in their jobs, their families, their churches, or in special ministry outlets."

Paul understood passion, for his personal passion had strengthened him to willingly accept all kinds of distress, loss, and rejection for the gospel. His passion motivated him to go to the hardest places, whether it meant a course change to Macedonia, remaining on a sinking ship, or boldly standing before the rulers of the land. He entered prisons and cast out demons in the name of Christ. In fact, the church council at Jerusalem sent Paul and Barnabas to Antioch with a letter that described them as having "risked their lives for the sake of our Lord Jesus Christ" (Acts 15:26).

Paul knew that passion is the result of serving with God's strength, for it is then that we can take hold of our ministry and see it through with victorious results. Paul called us to serve in the same way that a runner competes in a race—to win! "Do you not know that in a race that runners all compete, but only one receives the prize? Run in such as way that you may win it" (1 Corinthians 9:24).

Winning the race requires a passionate commitment to serve with God's strength. Failing to minister in this way is failing to run the race. We won't reach the finish line, much less win the prize. The needs of the world will go unmet. The lost will remain lost. The sick will die. The imprisoned will stay bound. And most important, our part of God's plan will have to be handled by someone else.

Paul also understood that we are not competing against others, but against the unseen enemies of Christ, those who would distract us or hinder us in any way from pouring ourselves into God's service with all of our heart, mind, soul, and strength. Just as Paul lived passionately committed to ministry, so we are to be passionately intentional in our commitment to meet the needs of people, whatever and wherever they may be, not in our own strength, but with God's.

Serving with God's Strength

Why do we have needs in the world? While I don't know the answer to this question, I do believe that God is often able to reveal His divine power, healing, and hope through His people where there is need. You have been gifted to minister, to meet the needs of people intentionally. How will you minister today?

LEADING WITH GOD:
Leadership

*A*fter he had washed their feet, had put on his robe, and had returned to the table, he said to them, "Do you know what I have done to you? You call me Teacher and Lord—and you are right, for that is what I am. So if I, your Lord and Teacher, have washed your feet, you also ought to wash one another's feet. For I have set you an example, that you also should do as I have done to you."

—John 13:12–15

LEADING WITH GOD

When a successful figure becomes especially prominent and conspicuous, the majority give way to the idolization of success.

—Dietrich Bonhoeffer, *Ethics*

Jesus calls us to be prominent and conspicuous, but not according to the world's standard for success. Rather, He calls us to a success that turns people to God. "'You are the light of the world. A city built on a hill cannot be hid. No one after lighting the lamp puts it under the bushel basket, but on the lampstand, and it gives light to all in the house. In the same way, let your light shine before others, so that they may see your good works and give glory to your Father in heaven'" (Matthew 5:14–16).

Perhaps you have not recognized this verse as a comment on leadership, but according to Jesus, those who trust Him are indeed leaders. We are the light of the world! And the world is watching us to see how our light shines.

Knowing this, Jesus admonished us to be aware of the Light that shines through us, and to use it to influence others toward God. We are leaders, whether we admit to it or not, with great potential for good works and spiritual leadership. Matthew 5:14–16 affirms that all followers of Christ are leaders and are to let their "light shine before others, so that they may see your good works and give glory to your Father in heaven."

Parents influence their children, siblings influence their brothers and sisters, children influence their peers, workers influence their co-workers, friends influence their friends. Leading with God is the Christian's call to influence family, friends, co-workers, and even strangers toward God.

One day, when my daughter was in her early teens, she was babysitting the little boy next door. I was at home and happened to overhear her correcting him. When I heard her words and tone of voice, they were mine! She was learning from me how to talk and "mother." As I listened to her, I was awakened to the power of my words and actions in my daughter's life.

Who is in your path of influence? Where are you leading? Are you leading with God and to God? Jesus intends that all who call Him Lord lead others to God through their life and works. He calls all Christ followers to an intentional leadership.

INTENTIONAL LEADERSHIP

Leading with God is intentional leadership. Yet it is not about positions and titles. While some are given the gifts for "forms of leadership," which would include formal leadership roles (1 Corinthians 12:28), intentional leadership includes those who live and walk in such a way that they influence others toward God and His purposes for the world.

Ken Blanchard, author of *The One Minute Manager* and founder of the Center for FaithWalk Leadership, defines a leader as anyone who influences another. Many believers do not see themselves as leaders because they do not hold a formal leadership position or have a recognized leadership title. They haven't awakened to the reality that they are indeed called to lead others to God. They haven't recognized the opportunity they have to lead with God.

When I think of people who have influenced me, I quickly realize their influence came from who they are, not from their position or title. The most influential people in my life are my family and my friends, people so near to me that their potential to influence is powerful.

Leading with God is the intentional decision to use

our influence to turn others toward God. The gospel depends on women and men who choose to lead like God, for it is only this kind of leading that can equip the next generation for God's purposes. A common passage from Deuteronomy calls us to this focused approach to leading.

> *Hear, O Israel: The Lord is our God, the Lord alone.*
> *You shall love the Lord your God with all your heart,*
> *and with all your soul, and with all your might. Keep*
> *these words that I am commanding you today in your*
> *heart. Recite them to your children and talk about them*
> *when you are at home and when you are away, when you*
> *lie down and when you rise. Bind them as a sign on your*
> *hand, fix them as an emblem on your forehead, and write*
> *them on the doorposts of your house and on your gates.*
>
> —Deuteronomy 6:4–9

Leading with God begins in our homes and extends into the world, wherever we go. We are called to an influence that comes from loving God with our entire being. Such influence transforms homes, lives, and societies.

A FEW BIBLICAL PICTURES FOR LEADING WITH GOD

"You are the light of the world" and "Bind [these words] as a sign on your hand" are two metaphors for biblical influence. Scripture provides powerful pictures for leading with God. These are metaphors for every believer who chooses to live for God's purposes, for every believer who chooses to be intentional in influencing others toward God's purposes.

Wash One Another's Feet

At the heart of our influence is our commitment to servanthood. Jesus commanded His followers to adopt a servant attitude for life and leading.

So if I, your Lord and Teacher, have washed your feet, you also ought to wash one another's feet. For I have set you an example, that you also should do as I have done to you.

—John 13:14–15

But he said to them, "The kings of the Gentiles lord it over them; and those in authority over them are called benefactors. But not so with you; rather the greatest among you must become like the youngest, and the leader like one who serves."

—Luke 22:25–26

A leader can take others only to places where they themselves have been. Henry Blackaby writes in *Spiritual Leadership*, "The greatness of an organization will be directly proportional to the greatness of its leader." For those who lead with God, greatness comes through servanthood. We bow before God, giving way to His greatness. We can't "lord" over others, for we know that we are completely under the lordship of Christ. He is Lord and we are His servants. His greatness enables us to influence others toward His purposes. In other words, influencing others toward God's purposes calls for a greatness that comes through serving.

When Jesus washed the disciples' feet, He was "commissioning" them to serve. Throughout His life He modeled servanthood. When He said, "Do as I have done," I believe He had much more in mind than just washing feet. Rather, He was calling them to follow the example of His life. Just as He had served them by giving Himself away to the needs of others, so now they were to serve in the same way.

Deny Yourself

Leading with God means serving like Jesus. We begin by giving up our personal power. Even Jesus, the greatest leader of all time, took on the form of a slave (Philippians 2:6–8). He gave up His personal power, submitting entirely to God's power. Jesus knew how to handle power, but few of us can handle power effectively. Power can take on a life of its own, even become a goal that undermines the effectiveness of God's power in our lives.

Janet O. Hagberg, in *Real Power: Stages of Personal Power in Organizations*, helps us to identify the various ways we tend to use power. See if you can identify healthy approaches to power. Do you recognize your own use of power in any of these?

Powerlessness: When we feel powerless, we often resort to manipulation of others. We undermine our relationships and devalue the freedom of others. We dishonestly influence others.

Power by association: If we are uncertain about who we are or about our own values, we may "copy" what others do, choosing to be seen with the right people, or adopting certain practices that seem to increase esteem and influence. We artificially influence others.

Power by achievement: We may find our power in title and position. We depend on these to keep control, whether the position is in the church, in the community, or in the workplace. Titles can be dangerous achievements when our goal is personal power. Our titles influence others.

Power by reflection: We may gain power from our

own value system and the way it is lived out through our lives. Our credibility influences others.

Power by purpose: If we know who we are and what we are about, we are able to give away power, and as a result we empower others. Our vision influences others.

Power by wisdom: We can affirm our limited ability by turning to a greater power for increased understanding and wisdom. We can humble ourselves before God, and our humility influences others.

> *Leading with God requires giving up our own power to allow God's power to work through us.*

You probably identified reflection, purpose, and wisdom as being healthy approaches to power, and ones that can lead to godly influence; yet few of us fully let go of our need to be in control. We fear giving away our authority. We enjoy our positions and titles. We forget that the only significant power is that which comes from God.

Leading with God requires giving up our own power to allow God's power to work through us. For intentional leaders, power is a gift from God. Any power of value is God's power at work through His people to transform lives. Paul prayed for the Christians in Ephesus that they would know "what is the immeasurable greatness of his power for us who believe, according the working of his great power" (Ephesians 1:19). To the church at Colossae he wrote, "For this I toil and struggle with all the energy that he powerfully inspires within me" (Colossians 1:29). Intentional leaders have a supernatural power, an enabling power for leading others toward God's purposes.

Take Up Your Cross

We need the supernatural power of God, for He calls us to the "front line" of ministry. Jesus said, "'I am sending you out like lambs into the midst of wolves'" (Luke 10:3). The front line is where we encounter trouble and persecution because we are representing the righteousness and justice of God in the world.

The front line is where we will stand against the major *fault lines* of oppression and injustice that exist in the world. Fault lines are precipices of lostness, loneliness, and hatred. Fault lines may be found as close as our own church community and the surrounding urban context where people, poverty, wealth, crime, politics, and all other spiritual and social issues exist. In other words, front line places are where Jesus is found working and seeking those who will join Him in the hardest places of life, the places that are often resistant to God's goodness, where tension and disagreement often occur.

Leading with God is a call to conflict, misunderstanding, and resistance, for the forces of this world hate the transforming power of God at work. Even so, we can stand with assurance that God will do what we cannot do when we take up our cross to lead with Him. He will work through us to bring transformation. Our world will be changed. We will be changed. We will become the presence of God to a hurting world.

Martin Luther King wrote in his "Letter from Birmingham Jail":

> *I think I should indicate why I am here in Birmingham, since you have been influenced by the view which argues against "outsiders coming in." . . . I am in Birmingham because injustice is here. Just as the prophets of the eighth century B.C. left their villages and carried their "thus saith the Lord" far beyond the boundaries of their home towns, and just as the Apostle Paul left his village of Tarsus and carried the gospel of Jesus Christ to*

the far corners of the Greco-Roman world, so am I compelled to carry the gospel of freedom beyond my own home town. Like Paul, I must constantly respond to the Macedonian call for aid.

Most would agree that Birmingham is a far better place today because King chose to lead with God. He faced conflict, misunderstanding, and resistance, but because he knew God's power was greater than his own, he gained strength to take up his cross and stand for the rights of those who could not stand for themselves.

A couple I know moved with their two children to a remote African village where the water and electricity we take for granted are barely accessible. "Taking up their cross" meant giving up the contemporary conveniences. Yet because they have chosen to lead with God, they are being transformed into the image of Christ. They rely on the supernatural power of God to fill them with love for the people, giving them strength to stand at the fault line year after year, bringing hope where few would care to visit, much less live.

Whether taking up our cross leads us to our own backyard or across the world, leading with God will always include taking up our cross. In this way, our influence will not only bring transformation, but will also influence others to hear God's call to take up their cross.

Filled with the Holy Spirit
Washing feet, denying self, and taking up our cross daily aren't typical responses. The good news is that we don't have to do these things on our own. Scripture calls us to let God do it for us, through His Spirit that abides in us. "And the disciples were continually filled with joy and with the Holy Spirit" (Acts 13:52 NASB).

Intentionally following Jesus is a life lived in the Spirit, for the Spirit teaches about, guides toward, and points to God and God alone.

> *For those who are according to the flesh set their minds on the things of the flesh, but those who are according to the Spirit, the things of the Spirit. For the mind set on the flesh is death, but the mind set on the Spirit is life and peace, because the mind set on the flesh is hostile toward God; for it does not subject itself to the law of God, for it is not even able to do so, and those who are in the flesh cannot please God.*
>
> —Romans 8:5–8 (NASB)

J. Oswald Sanders writes in his book *Spiritual Leadership*, "Spiritual leadership requires Spirit-filled people. Other qualities are important; to be Spirit-filled is indispensable." He describes this kind of leadership as "controlled by the Spirit. The Christian leader's mind, emotions, will, and physical strength all become available for the Spirit to guide and use. Under the Spirit's control, natural gifts of leadership are lifted to their highest power, sanctified for holy purpose."

The Holy Spirit teaches and empowers us for leading with God.

SELF-EVALUATION FOR INTENTIONAL LEADERS

Leading with God assumes dependence on God. We admit we need help in gaining the kind of influence we desire. Rather than looking for faults in someone else when we don't have the influence we want, we should examine ourselves. Self-reflection and self-examination become a lifelong commitment, as we rely on God to show us truths about ourselves that only He can see clearly.

Have you noticed your ability to see clearly can change if you go from bright light to dim? God views us in bright light. Psalm 139 reminds us that there is no darkness in God: "Even the darkness is not dark to you." This is why the psalmist prayed, "Search me, O God, and know my heart; test me and know my thoughts. See if there is any wicked way in me, and lead me in the way everlasting" (Psalm 139:23–24). The psalmist understood that self-reflection is of value only when God is involved.

God often uses life experiences to awaken us to a thought pattern, or an attitude, or a behavior that is out of line with His purposes. He seeks to open our eyes to assumptions that keep us from fully exploring and fulfilling His mission. Can you recall how God has used situations like the following in your life?

• You had an upsetting and unexpected experience that challenged your beliefs.

• You listened to someone tell of a similar experience to yours, which provided a new way to look at your own experience.

• You watched how someone behaved and changed your own behavior.

Scripture includes many examples of assumptions that interfere with God's purposes. In 2 Kings 5, the story is told of Naaman, an army captain who had leprosy. He was told by the prophet Elisha to wash in the Jordan River seven times and he would be healed. Naaman's assumptions almost kept him from being healed. First, he already had his mind set on how he thought his healing should take place. Second, he felt the Jordan River was not satisfactory for him. What he didn't understand is that his healing was a gracious act of God. His healing was about obedience, not about the river water or the method used.

His assumptions blinded him to his own need, and to the ways that God works in the world.

Leading with God is an intentional decision to challenge our assumptions, attitudes, and beliefs in order to provide the best leadership possible. God has equipped us with our textbook, His Word, and He has blessed us with all the gifts and skills we need to transform lives through our leading. The more we study our textbook and respond to the teaching of the Holy Spirit, the greater the potential for transformed lives. The more our assumptions and values are in line with God's mission, the more fruit our ministry will bear.

INTENTIONAL LEADERS ARE CHRIST FOLLOWERS

Leading with God is the natural outcome of being a follower of Christ. We may think of ourselves as weak and ineffective, but when we awaken to the reality of God's power at work through us, we see our lives differently. We view the way we follow Jesus differently, intentionally—choosing to live for God's purposes alone, just as Jesus did. His desires become our desires. We discover the influence of being a Christ follower.

All of us are followers of someone, and we all have people who follow us. People follow people for lots of different reasons. In *Leadership 101*, John C. Maxwell suggests that people follow leaders because:

- They have to.
- They want to.
- They like what someone's done for the organization they lead.
- They like what someone's done for them.
- They like who someone is and what they stand for.

Of all the reasons listed above, why do you follow Jesus? Following Jesus into the hard places of leadership—

the places out of our comfort zones, the places with high levels of personal risk—requires a unique kind of follower, the kind who follows Jesus because of who He is. When we follow Jesus because of who He is and because of God's love for us, we will be more likely to become exemplary followers.

What does an exemplary follower look like? In the book *Insights on Leadership* edited by Larry Spears, contributor Robert E. Kelley provides a list of attributes found in exemplary followers:

They know how to lead themselves well. They can be trusted with their responsibilities. No one has to remind them of their accountabilities. They discipline their lives, making the most with the time and resources they have been given.

They have focus, commitment, and incentives beyond personal gain. Their high enthusiasm is infectious to the organization. They are living with a sense of purpose that brings value to others.

They build competence and credibility to have maximum influence in the workplace. They have higher competency standards for themselves than those of the general work environment. Rather than judging others, they are concerned with their own commitment to excellence.

They exercise an honest, courageous conscience when carrying out assignments and implementing policies. The ethics of their actions are important to them. When faced with an ethical dilemma, the decision for how to respond has already been made, for they live by a set of values that guides their daily choices.

They control their own egos to work cooperatively with other leaders. They do their homework and argue persuasively without being threatening or self-righteous. Others would describe them as humble and accepting.

Kelley writes that we spend up to 90 percent of our

time following. But Christians are followers of Christ 100 percent of our time. As we think of following Jesus into the hard places of life and becoming exemplary followers, we must ask ourselves:

- Can He trust me enough to delegate His mission into my hands?
- Is my passion for His mission infectious to those around me?
- Am I transformed enough to accomplish my part of His mission?
- Does His mission so engage my life that I can be completely transparent before others?
- Is my only desire that His mission be accomplished?

We seek to transform the world around us, but we can only do so if we ourselves are transformed by God. Such transformation comes as we become exemplary followers of Christ.

Following Jesus Is Costly

When we decide to live intentionally for our "holy purpose," we can also know that we will pay a cost. Jesus assured us that He will be with us, and that He will help carry the burden of our purpose, but that an intentional following of Him will require a life commitment.

He called the crowd with his disciples, and said to them, "If any want to become my follower, let them deny themselves and take up their cross and follow me. For those who want to save their life will lose it, and those who lose their life for my sake, and for the sake of the gospel, will save it. For what will it profit them to gain the whole world and forfeit their life? Indeed, what can they give in return for their life? Those who are ashamed of me and of my words in this adulterous and

*sinful generation, of them the Son of Man will also be
ashamed when he comes in the glory of his Father with
the holy angels."*

—Mark 8:34–38

Today we face the same "adulterous and sinful generation" mentioned by Jesus in Mark 8. Only in following
Jesus will we be able to let go of our lives to be the servant leaders needed in today's world. What does servant
leadership look like?

Servant leaders find joy in giving over getting.

Servant leaders add value to everything they do.

Servant leaders feel connected to the peoples of the
world.

Servant leaders expect great things to come.

Servant leaders depend on God.

Jesus said:

*"You are my friends if you do what I command you. I
do not call you servants any longer, because the servant
does not know what the master is doing; but I have
called you friends, because I have made known to you
everything that I have heard from my Father. You did
not choose me but I chose you. And I appointed you to
go and bear fruit, fruit that will last, so that the Father
will give you whatever you ask him in my name. I am
giving you these commands so that you may love one
another."*

—John 15:14–17

Jesus calls us to a new kind of leading that loves people,
sacrifices self, follows Jesus, and pleases God.

The Intentional Follower's Destination

Christ followers have a destination that begins with our commitment to follow Him. His first disciples discovered this when Jesus came to them and said, "Follow me." He emphasized that simple commandment again and again, and in the last hours of His time on earth, He spelled it out again.

> *"Go therefore and make disciples of all nations, baptizing them in the name of the Father and of the Son and of the Holy Spirit, and teaching them to obey everything that I have commanded you. And remember, I am with you always, to the end of the age."*
>
> —Matthew 28:19–20

Our destination is to follow Jesus in making disciples, whether in the marketplace, the schoolroom, the boardroom, or the home. We have been sent and we have been entrusted with the mission that began *in Christ*. Without a doubt, leading like God is to follow Jesus into the world.

A WORD ABOUT THE POTENTIAL OF WOMEN LEADING WITH GOD

The New Testament tells us that women were among those who followed Jesus. Scripture also tells us of women who influenced others toward God's purposes. Jesus invited women to participate in His mission and called them along with men to let their light shine before others.

Even so, I have come to realize that women often underestimate their power to influence. They often do not see themselves as having potential to become God's leaders wherever they are. Yet, when their nurturing nature is combined with selflessness, they gain an attitude and commitment that lifts others to God and His purposes. Such nurturing, such influence is an *intentional* approach to the way they relate to their families, their friends, and others in their realm of influence. Jesus Himself was a nurturing leader who selflessly pointed people to His Father. Women can be true Christ followers when they intentionally lead in this Christlike way.

Carol E. Becker in her book *Leading Women* explores the potential of women as leaders and identifies qualities often found in the way that women influence those around them. Since I have seen these same qualities in many of the Christian women I meet, I've taken Becker's list and addressed these from a Christian perspective. The influence potential is exciting to think about!

Women care how the job is done. As Christians, we are uniquely gifted to care as much about how a task impacts people as we are about completing the task. We are also in a good place to be ethical and honest about the way a task is done. We care as much about *how* we accomplish a task as we care about the final result.

Women care about the whole person. We tend to care about the physical, spiritual, and emotional issues involved. We don't segment the different elements of a person or a situation, but tend to look at all the aspects involved. Our goals are not only for successful completion of the project but also for the benefit of those involved.

Women care about working as a community. One important business leader states that he wouldn't have a leader in his company who worked and made decisions without input from others. He values collaborative leadership. When we lead with another person or a group of persons, we are equipping others for leading. As Christians, we can take others with us by coleading Bible studies, venturing into ministry together, taking missions trips together, and sharing our faith together. We can involve others in praying with us and planning with us, and implementing our plans together. At home, we can include our children in learning to worship and study and clean and cook and plan and have fun. Everything we do in our homes to bring honor to God should be passed along to another generation, whether it is a tradition, a spiritual habit, or a general commitment to God's purposes.

> *Women often underestimate their power to influence. They often do not see themselves as having potential to become God's leaders wherever they are.*

Women are relational. When I came to leadership as publisher for New Hope, I received from my new administrative assistant a wonderful sheet of paper that let me know a little about each of the staff with whom I would soon be working. I was pleased to discover that I would be working with people who care about people, and believe in the value of relationship and communication. Since arriving, I've discovered an incredibly mature group of believers who know how to express themselves honestly and openly, and still maintain their relationships. This has been one of the greatest blessings for me as a new member of their team.

Women are intimate, making them more willing to be vulnerable and more approachable in their leadership. I've observed leaders who keep a distance between themselves and others, and I've observed those who are tearing down all barriers to bring people together toward a common goal. My heart's desire is to lead in the latter way. I have been blessed to be in churches and in workplaces with women believers who are not afraid to engage in an intimate relationship. When women are willing to be vulnerable and also focused toward God's purposes, it opens the door to discuss the issues that impact the kingdom with honesty and integrity. We can hold one another accountable for bringing honor to God in the way we live and work.

Women are willing to take a risk. Women risk commitment. They risk acceptance and forgiveness. They open their homes to strangers. Women are not afraid to change their life situation to embrace another who is in need. Throughout history, women have often stood against social injustices. Recently, a leading Christian women's organization in Alabama decided to speak out against legislation that would legalize the lottery. Their voices, along with those of leading citizens in the state, effectively stopped the legislation from being approved. Women have been vocal in speaking against war, violence, abuse, addictions, and many other social ills that destroy people's lives, as well as families and children.

Women, along with men, who lead with God gain influence as well as vision for what God would have done in the world.

INFLUENCE AND VISION

God has the vision for our lives and our world. Only as we gain His vision can we effectively influence others toward His purposes. In *Spiritual Entrepreneurs*, Michael Slaughter tells of coming to Ginghamsburg Church as their new pastor in April of 1979. One chilly morning soon after arriving, he went out on the lawn behind the church and prayed, "Lord, I am not going to leave this field until I have a clear sense of your mission for this church." And so he remained to wrestle and not let go until he had a resolve concerning God's direction. He was there all day, and God spoke. Slaughter knew that only God had the plan for his church. Intentional leaders know that only God knows how His people can be transformed to a "radical commitment to the mission of God." Influence and vision are essential to leadership and come only as we do as Slaughter did—remain before God until we hear Him speak.

God has the vision for divine influence. J. Oswald Sanders quotes Hudson Taylor in his book *Spiritual Leadership*: "It is possible to move men, through God, by prayer alone." Sanders makes the point that great leaders are great pray-ers and writes, "The spiritual leader should outpace the rest of the church, above all, in prayer." Sanders explains that prayer quickens not only the spirit, but also the mind and body. Jesus Himself gained vision and divine influence from God through prayer.

> *In Jesus we discover that every believer has the potential for divine influence, the influence that can turn a heart or a nation to God's purposes.*

Jesus is our model of vision and influence. Every action He took came from His intimate communion with God. He showed through His life that even a casual conversation becomes transformational when we are leading with God. One beautiful story is of Zacchaeus, the tax collector. Who would have dreamed that Zacchaeus would leave a position that brought him power and wealth to follow Jesus? Not only did he follow Jesus, he decided to repay double all that he had taken. How many lives through the years have been influenced by this story of a man transformed? The awesome realization for us is that God can work through us to achieve this same level of transformation when we choose to lead with God. Jesus showed us again and again the power of our lives when we gain our vision and influence through an intimate relationship with God.

Jesus was the highest-level leader, relying on the highest of all power, to influence others toward a radical involvement in the mission of God. He is our model. In Him we see how to lead with God. In Him we discover that every believer has the potential for divine influence, the influence that can turn a heart or a nation to God's purposes.

Nothing is more rewarding than leading with God. In their book *Spiritual Leadership*, Henry and Richard Blackaby address the rewards of leadership. They conclude their book with these words:

> *Moving people on to God's agenda is an exhilarating endeavor. Helping people grow, mature, and gain new skills is immensely gratifying. Taking weak, ineffective organizations and transforming them into robust, productive enterprises brings tremendous satisfaction. Nevertheless, such leadership does not come arbitrarily. People do not become spiritual leaders haphazardly. They become leaders through the opportunities the Holy Spirit provides as they strive to become the kind of people God desires them to be. Effective leadership results from hard work and a continuing effort to learn.*

Leading with God is hard work, but it brings the greatest of all rewards—participating with God in the fulfillment of His purposes. Leading with God is the natural outcome of choosing to live for God's purposes. This is intentional living!

Leading with God
"Make me to know your ways, O LORD; teach me your paths. Lead me in your truth, and teach me; for you are the God of my salvation; for you I wait all day long" (Psalm 25:4–5). Leading with God means following Jesus. How will you lead someone to follow Jesus today?

Conclusion

Intentional Living

As believers in Christ, we who live intentionally will influence others toward God's purposes.

- Our spirituality will encourage others to worship God.
- Our understanding of Scripture will open the minds of others to discover God's mission.
- Our view of the world will free others to see God's love for all people.
- Our relationships will be an invitation to cross barriers for Christ.
- Our communication will reveal Jesus through our lives and words.
- Our ministry will give assurance that Jesus is relevant to everyday life.
- Our leadership will influence others to choose to live for God's purposes.

Such intentionality calls for attentiveness to the Holy Spirit at work in our life. We choose again and again to respond to God's voice. Our continuing response results in an intentional commitment to God's purposes. The Apostle Peter confirmed the truth of Jesus Christ and His coming again. He assured us that the prophetic message of Christ's coming is indeed true. Then Peter wrote these words: "You will do well to be attentive to this as to a lamp shining in a dark place, until the day dawns and the morning star rises in your hearts" (2 Peter 1:19).

This verse, one of my favorites, is Peter's admonition to us to live with intentionality, to live every moment in expectation of the coming of our Lord. Intentional living is all about letting your lamp shine in a dark place "until the day dawns and the morning star rises in your hearts."

PASSING ON THE PASSION!

Intentional living is a passionate way of life. We can hardly wait to see what God will do in our lives and in the lives of others. We anticipate His amazing work in our communities and around the world. When we choose to live intentionally, we look forward to seeing how those around us, even the next generation, are influenced to a deliberate commitment to God's purposes.

Intentional living results in passing the passion for God's mission from generation to generation. When my granddaughter Chelsea was 6, I was seated next to her at my daughter's home. We were reading a book together. She said, "Grandmommy, when I grow up I want to go all over the world and tell others about Jesus just like you do." Her words surprised me, since I had never thought about what I do in those terms. I remember thinking, "Whatever it is she sees in my life, O Lord, let me live in such a way that she will continue to describe my life with these words." Recently, when I mentioned this to Chelsea, now 14, she said she could remember it clearly— down to what she was wearing and how she had her hair done!

You see, God has already intentioned her life for His purposes. Now it is up to her and those of us who have the opportunity to help shape her future to prepare her for God's intentional plan. Our passion for God's purposes will inspire her and others to discover God's plan for them. Our passion for God's mission may yield a new generation of passionate believers committed to living intentionally.

We have the honor of passing on the passion, an intentional decision to live for God's purposes!

Now to him who by the power at work within us is able to accomplish abundantly far more than all we can ask or imagine, to him be glory in the church and in Christ Jesus to all generations, forever and ever. Amen.

—Ephesians 3:20–21

GROUP
DISCUSSION GUIDE

U SE THE SHORT OUTLINES BELOW as a beginning point for discussion. Engage in discussion that leads toward a more intentional approach to living for God's purposes. Keep a journal of your discoveries and your commitments. Spend time in prayer for one another. At the end of the nine weeks, guide each participant to commit to involvement in God's mission.

Session One—Intentional Living
• Pray that each participant will choose to live for God's purposes.
• Explain the meaning of intentional living.
• Read John 17:15–18 and discuss the importance of why we live, how we live, and where we live in regard to God's purposes.

Session Two—Prepared for Intentional Living
• Read John 17:15–18 again.
• Discuss the four ways God prepares us for intentional living.
• Share stories of how these four preparations have been evident in the lives of the group members.

Session Three—Embracing God's Character
• Pray that each participant will seek a missional spirituality.

- Discuss three spiritual disciplines that are key to intentional living.
- Read Philippians 2:8–11 and discuss how Jesus' obedience furthered God's mission.

Session Four—Thinking with God's Mind
- Pray that each participant will understand the mission of God.
- Read Luke 24:46–49 and discuss the overall message of the Bible.
- Lead the group to make a list of ways that we bless others.

Session Five—Seeing Through God's Eyes
- Pray that each participant will choose to see as God sees.
- Read Jeremiah 5:1,3–5 and discuss what it means to have a worldview.
- Explain how we can test our assumptions and some intentional decisions that can help us see as God sees.

Session Six—Loving with God's Heart
- Pray that participants will be able to identify barriers in their own lives.
- Read 1 Corinthians 9:19–23 and discuss what Paul meant in this passage.
- List barriers that are common in our world and how these barriers can be overcome for the cause of the gospel.

Session Seven—Telling God's Story
- Pray that participants will be intentional in communicating Christ.
- Read or tell the story found in Mark 5:1–20. Discuss how this illustrates authentic evangelism.
- Ask group members to tell how Christ is at work in their lives.

Session Eight—Serving with God's Strength
- Pray that participants will discover their passion for ministry.
- Read Matthew 9:12–13 and discuss the way that Jesus has commanded us to respond to the needs around us.
- Ask group members to tell about their passion for ministry.

Session Nine—Leading with God and Conclusion
- Pray that participants will be intentional about the way they influence others.
- Read Matthew 5:14–16 and discuss how this relates to leadership.
- Discuss ways that we influence others toward God's mission.
- Read 2 Peter 1:19 and close by encouraging the group to intentionally let their light shine in a dark place until the day dawns and the morning star rises in their hearts.